The N.P.M.W.A.R.A.
The North Pacific Major World Air Route Area

By The Same Author

ISLANDS OF EXPERIENCE

A POET'S SKETCH
OF HIS BIOGRAPHY

KID ON THE RIVER

A SAILOR'S YARNS —
AND OBSERVATIONS

TWO CATS FOR PUERTO RICO

THE HIGHLINE TRAIL

ONE LIFE'S THREAD

THE COPPER SANDS
AND PRINCE WILLIAM SOUND

The N.P.M.W.A.R.A.

The North Pacific Major World Air Route Area

Dean Nichols

Resource *Publications*

An imprint of *Wipf and Stock Publishers*
199 West 8th Avenue • Eugene OR 97401

Resource Publications
A division of Wipf and Stock Publishers
199 W 8th Ave, Suite 3
Eugene, OR 97401

The N.P.M.W.A.R.A.
The North Pacific Major World Air Route Area
By Nichols, Dean
Copyright©1994 by Nichols, Dean
ISBN: 1-59752-281-3
Publication date 6/27/2005
Previously published by Binford & Mort Publishing, 1994

To
Margaret, and Wally,
and Jim, and Phyllis,
and Greg.

"The steps of a man are directed and established of the Lord..."

Ps. 37:23 Amp. Bible

Contents

Acknowledgements	ix
Prologue	xii
Drama in the Night Skies	1
The N.P.M.W.A.R.A	7
The Versatile Human Machine	13
Those Grand Old Birds	21
On the Beach	31
Re-earning My Wings	37
"The Steps of a Man..."	47
Odd Stories—Somewhat Related	57
Fam Trips—and Other Stories	71
Odd Stories—Heart of the Job	79
The Final Story	107
Epilogue	113
Glossary	115

Acknowledgements

I was trying to get two other books published and was stalling at writing this one. So I must give credit to my wife, Ramona, who, in that persuasive and unique way of a North Dakota, Swedish, farm girl, said, "Dean, *others* can publish your books; *only you* can write them."

So I hooked onto my Coachman travel trailer, drove to Bastendorff Beach Park on that jeweled, Oregon Coast, and wrote this book.

Dean Nichols

"For I dipt into the future, far as human eye could see, saw the vision of the world, and all the wonder that would be, saw the heavens filled with commerce, argosies of magic sails, Pilots of the purple twilight, dropping down with costly bales..."

Alfred Lord Tennyson
about 1860.

Prologue

The term, "Air Traffic Control" is a misnomer. They don't *control* anything. Oh, there will be screams, and invectives rise over that statement. But let's put some serious thought to that allegation.

How could a man on the ground control an aircraft 30,000 feet in the air, and hundreds of miles away? He couldn't, physically; he couldn't, morally; he couldn't lawfully, nor would the traditions, the wisdom of the ages, allow a man on the ground to usurp the sovereign authority of a captain on the bridge of his ship.

How then, does the air traffic system work?

Well, whether by accident, or on purpose, someone brilliantly came up with the term, "clearance." There must be order in the air—as on the sea, and on the highways. But how do we maintain order, and yet not undermine a captain's sovereignty?

The term, "clearance," carries a multiple connotation; or denotation, in this special case. When the controller says, "ATC clears..." he is, in essence, saying to the captain, "If you will maintain the altitude I say, and the course I say, Air Traffic Control will protect you in that block of airspace, from the invasion into that block by any other IFR (Instrument Flight Rules) aircraft. We will assume full responsibility for that protection."

But the other connotation? If the captain chooses, (and it is his full right to choose) to ignore the terms of the clearance, then by law, and, for that matter, by the years of tradition, the captain assumes full responsibility for whatever happens to that aircraft and any others he may bump into there.

For example: A Boeing 727 is on an approach to Philadelphia. He is some miles out, so not quite in the glide path/glide slope, but still, a quite narrowly restricted path. He breaks out of some clouds, and a thousand feet dead ahead, is a mean, mean thunderhead. It is clear a half mile on either side. There is no time to call ATC. To penetrate that thunderhead, with its obviously severe turbulence, could damage, or even destroy his ship, and living cargo.

He rolls that 727 to the left, around that thunderhead, and *then* he calls ATC, and *he* tells *them* what he did.

But with those rare, rare exceptions, captains routinely accept clearances, almost as if they were commands. But it is always his option.

Never, never, never must the sovereign captain of any ship surrender that option.

But the "System" actually works very well, and, for those privileged to work in its inner circles, is an exhilarating experience. This book tells that story.

I would urge any serious reader to study, just a bit at least, the glossary on the back pages of this book. It will make your reading much more fun.

And by the way, this *is* a true story. Every dramatic, or funny, or revealing episode, actually happened.

Dean Nichols

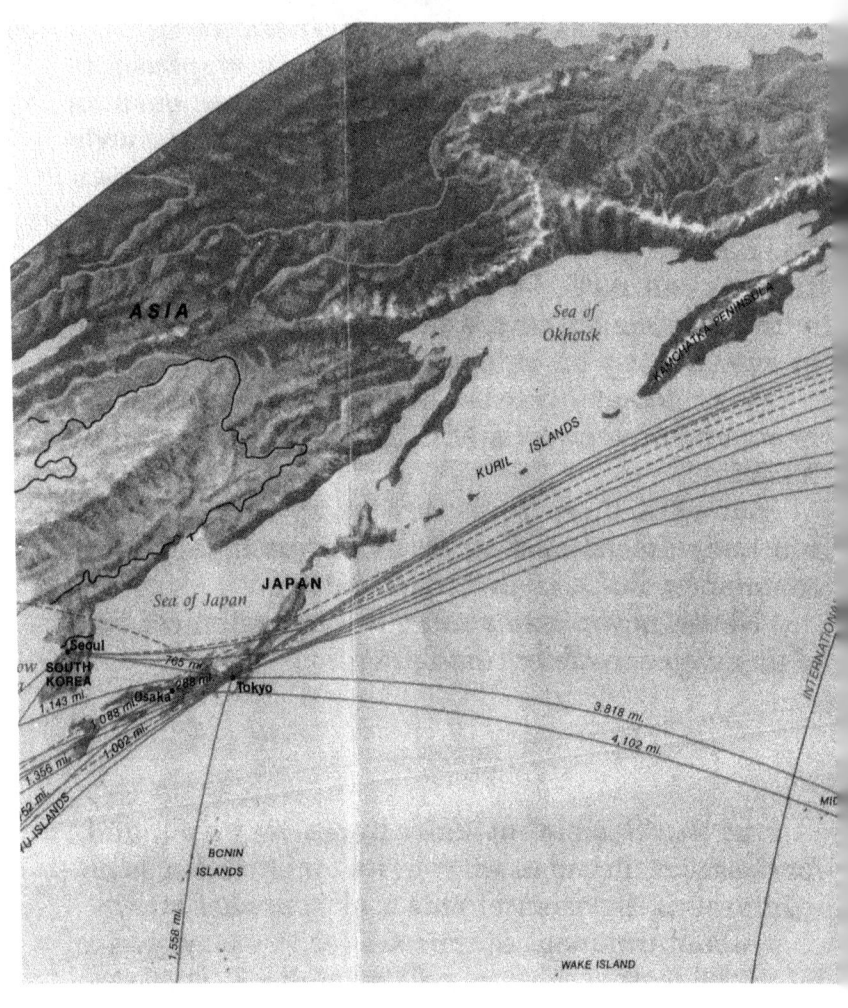

A portion of Northwest Airlines Route Map
indicating the approximate area of the N.P.M.W.A.R.A.

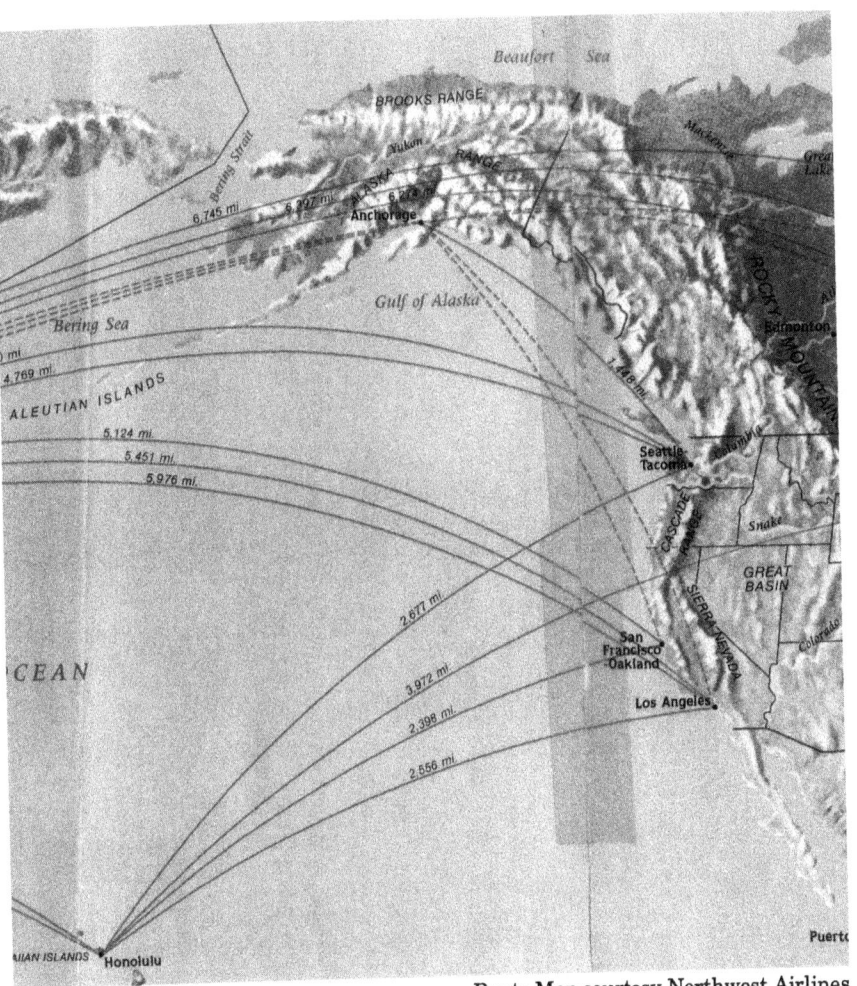

Route Map courtesy Northwest Airlines

CHAPTER 1

Drama in the Night Skies

The year is 1978. And high in that night sky, far out over the vast North Pacific Ocean, two Boeing 747s rush to their destinations. The several hundred passengers aboard the two jumbo jets doze and sleep on in their seats, blissfully unaware of the intense drama that is about to take place there, a drama that could touch, or even take their lives. Both aircraft are cruising at flight level 350 (approximately 35,000 feet.)

The cryptic, almost coded words of the actors in that drama, crackling through the radio waves, tell the story. An aircraft calls:

"Anchorage, NW 7." (Northwest Airlines, Flight 7.)

It had been a rapid fire, *busy* morning at ANC IFSS. (Anchorage International Flight Service [Radio] Station), but signals (the legibility of radio communications) had been good. I answered, "NW 7, Anchorage; go ahead."

"Anchorage, NW 7; we just accepted a clearance to 370 that was meant for NW 3. We are now at FL

370." (Roughly 37,000 feet.) That Boeing 747 was *not* supposed to be there.

(Above 18,000 feet, altitudes were expressed as FL, or flight levels. Above that altitude, all aircraft set their altimeters at a common setting, so that, even though their actual altitudes would vary with changing barometric pressure, the vertical separation *between* aircraft would be precise. It worked well. But that is just an explanation, not a point in this drama.)

I was a seasoned veteran by this time, so did not get shaken easily. Still, I was poignantly aware of the deadly seriousness of the intense drama being played out here. Air Traffic Control exists for the very purpose of keeping aircraft separated from each other. ATC *must* know where each aircraft is at all times. I turned to my assistant, manning the interphone to ATCC, the Air Traffic Control Center, "John, do you happen to have a clearance to 370 for NW 7?"

"Yes," he answered, "I'm getting it now," and handed me the blazing pink 5 x 7 sheet, with the cryptic message, "C NW 7 CTAM FL370. RR 370." (ATC clears NW 7, climb to and maintain FL 370. Report reaching 370.)

I called NW 7, and gave him the clearance. Immediately, the steady, clear voice responded, "NW 7 is cleared to 370. We are now at 370."

I don't know if that veteran, old captain of a NW Airlines, Boeing 747, was sweating or not. But the drama was not yet over.

I reached over to the "Suspense Board," and took the blazing pink slip that had the clearance for NW

3 written on it. It was time-stamped and initialled as having been duly delivered to NW 3.

"NW th-ree, Anchorage; Clearance."

I don't think I had time to breath a sigh of relief, but it was good to hear the strong, clear voice answer with the terse message: "NW 3, go."

"NW th-ree, Anchorage. ATC clears NW 3, CTAM FL 370. RL 350; RR 370." (Climb to and maintain FL370. Report leaving 350; report reaching FL 370.) And then I couldn't resist adding the unofficial admonition, "And, ah, expedite, please."

And from NW 3: "Anchorage; NW 3 is cleared to 370. We are leaving 350; will report reaching 370."

Photo courtesy Northwest Airlines

Should an author have favorites? Well, let the reader decide. A Northwest Airlines B-747 rules air so thin, a man could not breath, nor a bird fly, but where the jet belongs.

That pilot must have stood that Boeing 747 on its tail, for only moments later:
"ANC, NW 3 is level 370."
"NW 3, ANC; Roger, level 370." I resisted the temptation to speak into that microphone with, "Now be good, boys."

Instead, I turned to the two or three fellow Air Traffic Control Specialists in the radio room, and spoke with a deadly seriousness, "If *any* one, says *any* thing about this to *any* one, I will personally kill you."

It was never reported; nor need it have been. The aircraft were at their assigned flight levels, no one had been hurt; the erring pilots had been more than duly chastened by their own consciences, and that plus the fact that most of the other aircraft, scattered over the north half of the Pacific Ocean, had heard all also. A report to "Officialdom" would have resulted in weeks, or even months of investigation; pilots would have been embarrassed, perhaps even reprimanded far beyond any need; I would have been subjected to grilling that would have produced no useful result.

Coverup? I don't think so. Mankind is fallible; some human error will always appear, now and then. But in a finely tuned, highly skilled, intensely professional operation such as this, we had to, and did, correct for each other's errors. That is one of the reasons that you are six times safer riding a commercial airliner, than you are driving on the nation's freeways.

But what had happened? Well, without that investigation, we'll not know for sure. But most likely, the pilot of NW 7, or even the aircraft itself also, had been NW Flight 3 to Tokyo the day before. Both aircraft this day had requested to climb from FL 350 to FL 370. (Those guzzling jet engines burn much less fuel at higher altitudes. Their "MPG" goes up markedly up there. So as soon as they burn off enough fuel weight to allow it, they want to climb higher.)

When I had called, "NW 3, Anchorage; Clearance," NW 7, expecting a clearance, and forgetting, for a moment, that he was now NW 7, answered as NW 3, and accepted the clearance. And you know the rest of the story. I don't know why NW 3 missed the call.

The bad news? ATC, believing that NW 3 was climbing to FL 370, and NW 7 was still at FL 350, *could* have cleared another aircraft to cross 2000 feet under, or over one or the other, when in actuality, they would have crossed at the same altitude, and so *could* have collided.

The good news? There are millions of times more spaces in the sky the size of a B-747 than there are hunks of metal that size up there. And the odds are 10,000 to one, at least, that out over that vast ocean there would be no aircraft wanting to cross either flight path at that flight level, at that precise time.

But somehow, the drama of this event, in the night skies over the North Pacific Ocean, makes a story worth the telling.

CHAPTER 2

The N.P.M.W.A.R.A

The North Pacific Major World Air Route Area, reaches from well south of Seattle, up along the West Coast, includes Alaska, then west and southwest along the edge of Russia to Japan, and back across the Pacific Ocean on a line some north of the Hawaiian Islands. How many million square miles? Well, look at your own globe, and see the incredibly vast area over which thousands of flights occur, and yet for whom, their HF, (High Frequency) communications are handled by but two ground stations, Anchorage, Alaska, and Tokyo, Japan.

No, the story that follows will in no way be an exhaustive dissertation on the experiences of the men who manned the radio rooms of those two ground stations. A hundred times more stories could be told. But this truly, truly was a most dramatic period in my own life. It is my hope that the reader can experience at least a glimpse of that drama.

Anchorage, Alaska is often called, "The Air Crossroads of the world." Well, again, a look at your

Author photo
Anchorage International Airport. About 1965.

globe will show you why. And though that globe will show you that a shorter "Great Circle" route between Europe and Japan would be somewhere over Siberia, the Russian paranoia of the West will not allow such crossing. And Anchorage, with its industrious people, its shipping, its fuel and supply availability, its "halfway point," makes it a natural stopover for those "Polar Flights."

And the other "Great Circle" route from the Pacific Northwest to Japan, brought those flights over the shoulder of the globe, and so, close to Anchorage. Even the nonstop flights by PA (Pan American), and NWA (Northwest Airlines), from Chicago and New York to Tokyo, brought them over, or just north of Anchorage.

In the early days of the "Paddle Wheelers," (Propeller driven aircraft, such as the venerable DC-7s and Connies) Anchorage was often a necessary refueling stop. But even now, with the long range jets, Anchorage, almost in the middle of it all, is yet the vital, long range communication link with Mother Earth, with Company Dispatch, with Air Traffic Control.

And Tokyo, with its industrious people, its shipping, its fuel and supply availability, its "entry point" to the Orient, makes it a natural "crossroads" as well. And so the N.P.M.W.A.R.A. grew into being.

But how could these two ground stations, half a world apart, communicate directly with each other, and with all those aircraft (sometimes 30 or 40) scattered, at any one time, out over that broad sea? The secret was the unique characteristics of the HF (High Frequency) radio transmissions used.

Without going into a technical discourse on radio transmission, let me just briefly outline the four basic groups of radio frequencies used. I am not an electronics expert, so I cannot "snow" you with technical data. But that uniqueness, peculiar to those HF frequencies we used, is very pertinent to these stories. So let me touch on this data.

Most old broadcast radio stations use, and still use LF, or Low Frequency in their transmission. They ranged in the hundreds of kilocycles per second. Next came HF, or High Frequency, which we used. We had five: 2910, 5589, 8939, 13264, and, 17505 kilocycles per second. Next came VHF or Very High Frequency, in the hundreds of thousands of kilocycles per second. Most of your familiar "FM" stations use VHF. And, generally, the Military use UHF, or ultra High Frequency, about double the VHF frequency numbers.

The LF frequencies reach long distances, but the bands are almost saturated with broadcast stations. VHF, and UHF, while providing relatively static-free reception, are generally, "line of sight," as a beam of light would be. Generally, they are limited to 40 to 100 miles, depending on the terrain; although I believe that two aircraft at 30,000 feet, and out over the ocean, might reach two to ten times that. The short range disadvantage of VHF and UHF, becomes an advantage, in that the same frequencies can be used over and over, without interfering with each other, as long as they are generally a hundred miles or more apart. Now, with satellite, and microwave relay, aircraft over land, can talk directly to a Company, or Traffic Control Center, anywhere in the U.S.

And one more thing: Although it is technically feasible for an aircraft to use VHF, or UHF directly to a satellite, 22,500 miles up, and so talk (by relay) to a station half a world away, it requires quite expensive equipment. Thus, the survival of the old standby, HF.

The advantages? Those HF transmissions would head off, say for Tokyo, and even curve with the earth, a little bit. But in a few hundred miles, because of the startlingly rapid curvature of the earth, they would find themselves heading off into the sky, to be lost forever—except for that unique characteristic.

There is a nebulous, but very real blanket around the earth called the Ionosphere, generally, a couple hundred miles up. It is made up of ionized particles that, for these peculiar, HF radio signals, act as a mirror, reflecting those signals, at an angle, back to the earth. The earth acts as another mirror, and reflects them, at an angle, back to the Ionosphere. I don't know how many times this might occur on a transmission to Tokyo, but on a rare instance, I have talked, from Anchorage directly to a Pan American World Airways aircraft on the ground at Narita Airport, in Japan. (Of course *we* talked regularly to Tokyo *Radio*, but they had huge antennas, and powerful amplifiers. The aircraft had only a fraction of that.)

Ah, but again, the bad news. That Ionosphere was a fickle friend. It would change altitude between day, and night; higher, I believe, in the day and lower at night. *Generally*, that change was fairly consistent, and so we could change frequencies as the dawn came, or as night fell. The lower frequencies worked better at night; the higher in the day.

But then, the Solar Storms (Sun spots). Intense, magnetic storms on the sun, they would greatly increase the "Solar Wind," streams of particles from the sun. As that Solar Wind blasted around the earth, it would wreak havoc with that lovely blanket, that mirror we needed so badly. Like a mirror, blasted by blowing sand, or even at times, blasted by a shotgun, it would, for moments, and sometimes for hours, refuse to do its work. Oh, that same disturbance, produced those glorious Northern Lights, but, as we all know, beauty can be deadly too.

Sometimes, an aircraft only miles away, could not hear us at all. And another, 2,000 to 10,000 miles away would hear us loud and clear. Sometimes two aircraft would be a hundred miles apart. We could hear one, but not the other. The other could hear us, but not the one. Some curious relays took place at those times, but the system moved on, the airplanes kept flying, and the passengers, dozing comfortably, and yes, safely in their seats, slumbered blissfully on, gently riding on the soft ribbon of the wind.

I remember one night, in the earlier days, when we read back every PSNRP (Position Report); the signals had been terrible, rapidly fading in and out, often right in the middle of a transmission. We would have to ask for repeats of portions, and fill in, to complete the message. It was hard work.

Suddenly, out of the blue (or black of night) came a call from a Pan American World Airways aircraft, PA-3. Pan American Pilots, the self-styled Prima Donnas of the airways, were not noted for patience or diplomacy.

Loud and clear, the clearly irritated voice barked, "Anchorage, Clipper 3."

"Clipper 3, Anchorage; go."

"Anchorage, Clipper 3; where in blazes have you been, ANC? I've been calling you for half an hour."

My nerves taught, my own patience thin, I snapped back, "Clipper 3, Anchorage; FYI (For your information) signals are very erratic tonight. This is the first time I've heard you. You are loud and clear now, GO AHEAD."

A somewhat subdued Captain gave his PSNRP.

I read back the PSNRP in rapid fire delivery, and with no little metal in my voice.

And then quietly from Clipper 3, "Readback OK. Clipper 3 out."

They really were good boys. I'd fly with Pan American any day.

CHAPTER 3

The Versatile Human Machine

But how did I, this old river rat, husband, father of three children, come to be sitting at a console, the size of a Boeing 747 flight deck, in a radio room in Anchorage, Alaska, and playing the role of half of the ground communications for commercial aircraft, over the North Pacific Ocean? Well, the Good Book says, "The steps of a man are ordered of the lord." And that is true. But what of the sequence of events?

For twenty some years, I had operated tugboats on the Columbia River and Puget Sound. Family ties kept us there; the love of the River kept us there.

One day, my wife and I realized that the tugs kept "Daddy" away too much. So I took a job, for a brief time, as an assistant electrical engineer in our home town. But there was no drama there. And in the meantime, our family ties were slowly severed as our parents, one by one, left this earthly life. We were free to listen to the call of those "Far-away-places-with-strange-sounding-names."

Also, in the meantime, I had bought an airplane, and had accumulated nearly a thousand hours of flying time. At the same time, FAA (The Federal Aviation Agency) was recruiting for their rapidly expanding airways system.

A simple, white card appeared in the mail, one day. It read, "You, being a pilot, must know someone with one of the three following qualifications for training as an Air Traffic Control Specialist..." And they listed the three.

One was, "Have 350 hours or more of flying time." My wife and I looked at each other, and agreed, "That's me." And so, in March of 1958, I left that unromantic job, and found myself paddling up the "Inside Passage," aboard an old Alaska Airlines DC-4 with six other passengers and a fiberglass runabout boat aboard.

Then followed a couple years or so in the Anchorage FSS, (Flight Service Station) working with the putt-putts, as we called the Pipers, Cessnas, Aeroncas, and other small planes. They needed weather, flight planning, and radio contact with the ground, as they wove their way around the peaks, and across the tundra plains, and over the thousands of lakes, and empty miles and miles of Alaska's wilderness. This work was not without its own drama; but my great love, after a traumatic break-in, was working with the big birds, and the truly professional men who flew them.

As I understand it, ARINC, the corporation owned by several airlines, to provide their private radio communications, found it, in about 1960, too expensive to supply the radio communications for the then sparse traffic over the North Pole and the North Pacific. I believe, for example, that JAL,

Japan Airlines, then had just two flights a week over Alaska, as did KLM, Royal Dutch Airlines, AFR, Air France, and SAS, Scandinavian Airlines System. Today, Japan Air alone, has over 90 flights a week in and out of ANC.

But as I said, in about 1960, ARINC asked FAA to take over. In about 1985 or '86, the business again became profitable, so ARINC took the business back again. I am a devout capitalist, but I can't help interjecting, in this case, the suggestion, "So much for the free enterprise system." But enough of that; this is a story of drama in the skies.

But in 1960, I didn't want any part of E-459, the code number for the new international air-ground FAA had taken over. Fact is, I was scared to death of it. So I stalled, and stalled.

Finally, one night, a crusty supervisor, Ed Jones, just assigned me to E-459. I hated him for it, but gulped, and sat down. The agony that followed was unnecessary, but it was real. But somehow, through my near panic, I learned, and as I learned, I began to realize that this was actually easier. The pilots were professional; there were clearly specified patterns, and we all knew and followed them. I was having a great time. And Ed Jones was right. I don't think that I ever gave him the thanks that he deserved.

But it was during this break-in period, that I developed a real appreciation for, almost an affection for Northwest Airlines Pilots. They were kind of laid back, sure, but gentle and patient. It seemed they knew they had a novice "on the other end of the line," and so were considerate and helpful.

Some years later, we met a NWA Stewardess, who became a family friend. I related to Barbie my earlier experiences, and my appreciation for those pilots. She smiled, and said, "Well, I can understand that. NWA, headquartered in St. Paul, had hired many Minnesota farm boys. And those farm boys, although intelligent and strong, were also kind and gentle. Yes, I can understand that."

Some fifteen years later, during my second stint at E-459, I found that, of course, many of those farm boys had retired. And, the financial squeeze had hit old veteran, NWA, so that their radio equipment maintenance left something to be desired. Still, NWA is an old friend.

Over the years of my life, I have been frequently amazed at what the human machine can learn to do, and do easily, which, under earlier observation, would have seemed impossible.

During the early sixties, the aircraft would call us before takeoff and request reporting times. And so we would give one, 00 and 30, another 05 and 35, and so, on around the hour. One time would be for his PSNRP and the other for OPNML (Operations Normal). Obviously, six aircraft would fill the hour. Oh, we would often fill in two or three more at say, 02 and 32; but 16 or 18 contacts, with maybe a dozen clearances, or requests for weather added, were about it. But we were really busy with those 25 to 30 contacts. Of course, we read back every PSNRP for confirmation, which took some time. But those 15 years later, I found myself often making over 60 contacts an hour. And I believe the record was some 72 in one hour. I never quite made that record, but 60+ an hour is better than one a minute. Still, when one's mind and body are fully skilled, and tuned, and ready, it was incredibly exhilarating. Can you imagine a professional tennis player, or skilled fencer hating his job?

But back to those early years. I don't remember just when the jets took over, probably around 1962. But one quiet night a humorous drama took place. Of course, I was safely on the ground, not up there trying to get a 100-ton airplane, loaded with a couple hundred passengers, and a hundred tons of fuel, 5000 miles across an ocean. Still, the humor was there.

At the time JAL and KLM had exactly the same schedule out of Anchorage, for whatever reason. There was always a bit of struggle to be the first one out. This night, JAL made it out first, with KLM on his tail. A couple hours later, KLM, at FL330, wanted FL350, but JAL was there. He waited. Finally, he requested FL370. I called ATC, and received:

"CA KL867, UN 370 due TFC." (ATC advises KL867, unable to clear you to FL370 due conflicting traffic—namely, JAL.)

"ANC, KL867."

"KL867, ANC. Go ahead."

"ANC, KL867, Request VFR (Visual Flight Rules) climb to FL370."

I knew that it was a crystal clear night, and that he could see the lights of JAL out ahead of him ten or 20 miles. But ATC came back with:

"CA KL867. VFR climb unauthorized at night."

The Dutch, like those Minnesota farm boys, are generally quite stable. But this Dutch boy was getting frustrated.

Finally, that Dutch accent thundered, "Anchorage, KL867. Do you mean to tell me that I have to fly the rest of the way across the Pacific Ocean at 33,000 feet, and burn five tons more of fuel, just on account of one aircraft?"

I felt for him; I really did, and should not have been grinning. But it was such an incongruous situation. I answered:

"Sorry, Captain, but that's what ATC has given us."

There was a period of silence. But I could almost hear those Dutch invectives ricocheting around the flight deck of that DC-10.

"ANC, KL867."

"KL867, ANC, Go ahead."

"ANC, KL867. Request permission to contact JAL on this frequency."

I granted the permission, and listened.

"JL304; KL867."

"KL867; JL304."

"JL304; KL867, can you climb to FL370?"

"Ah, standby."

And a few minutes later: "JL304 can climb to 370."

So I cut in and asked JL304 if he was requesting FL370.

"That is affirmative. JL304." (That last was a sort of adding a signature to an abbreviated transmission, lacking a formal callup.)

So I hit my interfone (no assistant, those days) and obtained the two clearances.

"Deliver the clearance to KL867, *after* JL304 reports leaving 350," ATC cautioned.

"Yes, of course," I answered, and went to work. And KLM, Royal Dutch Airlines, were able to save 4 or 5 tons of costly jet fuel on a flight to Tokyo, Japan.

And there, alone, at the huge console of E-459, I had a few moments to reflect and smile at the anomalies and contrasts of life. How different this was from running a tugboat on a dark and rainy night on the Columbia River, just a few years before. There, guiding that small tug and her tow down the surface of that historic waterway, the shoreline passing by at 4 or 5 miles per hour, I had hours to make a decision; and, no one else's problems to consider.

Here, were three nationalities, from nations half a world apart; and two huge aircraft, racing west at close to the speed of sound, and at over 30,000 feet, had problems that demanded decisions in minutes. I miss my tugs. But I would not have missed that drama in the skies for anything.

How versatile, this human machine.

CHAPTER

4

Those Grand Old Birds

My work at E-459, was divided two ways: By time; that is, from about 1960 to the middle of 1965, when the siren call of the sea led me back to my boats for awhile; and a second period, 1977 through 1980. More of that story later.

But the other division was the dramatic changeover from the "Paddle Wheelers," the propeller driven aircraft, to the jets. Those "Paddle Wheelers" were in the air nearly twice as long on each flight. And so we had those old DC-7s, and Connies, often for an entire watch. We'd actually get acquainted.

At the time, we were changing shifts at two-week intervals, with only one day off a week. Often, that would result in a "short changeover." For example, I had gotten off work at 4:00 P.M., one afternoon, dashed home for supper, and a few hours sleep, and back to work at midnight. The fellow I was relieving gave me the traffic. And there on the list was an old friend, and, curiously, a DC-7, by the name of NW 7. He was now down by Kodiak Island. I had worked him out of TYO the afternoon before I went home.

We stayed together for a few more hours, until he got within VHF range of Seattle, and said goodbye with something like:

"Anchorage, NW 7, we're going over to VHF now. Thanks for the help. See you next trip."

"NW 7, ANC; Roger, have a good rest. ANC out."

Another time, Capt "Bluie" Salmon, an Australian, flying for KLM, had been visiting at my home. As I recall, about 16 hours earlier, he had left for his hotel room to pack for his return flight to Holland. When I came to work at midnight, the operator on E-457, the HF radio position that handled the offshore Airway between ANC and SEA, hailed me. "Do you know a pilot for KLM?" he asked.

"Yes, I do," I answered, "Why?"

"Well, as you know," he explained, "Our frequency, 8871, is supposed to be low powered enough that we can barely reach Seattle. But we were having some terrible 'skip' tonight. All of a sudden I could hear KL868, calling Amsterdam." (Apparently, the frequency was used over again there, because ordinarily, the power was kept low enough that there should be no interference.) "Well," he continued, "Amsterdam never came up, so I called the aircraft, and asked if I could help."

" 'This is KL868. What Station is calling?' he asked."

"So I told him, 'Anchorage, Anchorage, Alaska.' "

Those Grand Old Birds

"And he answered, 'Oh, hi, ANC. No, we're OK. They'll come up pretty soon. But say hello to Dean Nichols for me.'"

An illegal transmission? Oh, yes, of course. But we never abused it. The terse, authorized transmissions, were so clinical, we had to slip a little humanity in once in a while. The higher "brass" wisely turned their heads.

But where had my friend, Bluie, been for those 16 hours? Well, the ship he took over was late coming in from TYO; there had been some delay getting out of Anchorage; and then the winds up over the North Pole, and Greenland, had been more adverse than forcast. They had been paddling along up there, over that icy desert, for around 12 hours. I think a tired crew was glad to be getting home.

But the endurance of those grand old ladies, the DC-7s? Well, I don't know their maximum, but pilots have told me that, if necessary, their three hour reserve for holding over a destination could be stretched to over six hours. "We'd be real light on fuel weight by then, of course," he would say, "so we'd increase the propeller pitch a bit, and throttle back to where you could *see* those props turning out there. They're grand, old birds."

The jets, I believe, carry only around a half hour reserve of fuel. Of course, that's around 250 miles. But even so, the decision to divert was usually made well before arrival. Fairbanks, 300 miles north of Anchorage, was often listed as an alternate.

But there was a quite personal reason why I hated to see those lumbering, old workhorses give way to the swift "thoroughbreds," the racing jets.

Flying west, against the prevailing winds, even a DC-7 had to make a refueling stop in Keflavik, Iceland. In Keflavik, was a "Duty Free" shop. One time, Bluie, or maybe Cor den Hoedt, a Dutch pilot friend, brought me a bottle of Drambui. I think it is $12 to $15 a bottle now, or maybe more. But as I recall, the boys said they could get it there for around a dollar, or maybe less. I loved it.

"Greatest thing in the world for nursing a sore throat," I told them. So that established a delightful pattern.

I remember one time, taking a PSNRP from KL867, somewhere up near the North Pole, on his way from Holland. Recognizing my voice, Cor asked, "How is the throat?"

"Oh, *pretty* good," I responded, "But I'm low on cough syrup."

"Yah, we take care uff dat. KL867."

There were some delightful, unofficial, fringe benefits to the job.

But while we're on the subject of the truly marvelous, mechanical engineering triumphs of those powerful, many-cylindered, reciprocal engines, on the old "Paddle Wheelers," we have to relate a few of the problems they produced.

Maintenance on the jets, I'm told, is a fraction of that on those reciprocal engines. Mechanically, at least, they are vastly simpler, less complicated. So we never had a "Maintenance Report" from a jet an hour or so out. But always with the propeller ships. Most of the time, it would be several items. Typical would be, "Number two engine, second row, number five cylinder, primary not functioning." Rarely did a

"Maintenance Report" read, "Aircraft OK for turnaround."

And the DC-7 had another problem that, though rarely, did appear on occasion: the runaway prop. The engineer would lose control of the propeller pitch on an engine, and the pitch would slowly flatten. The pressure of the wind the airplane itself was making would cause that propeller to speed up. That flat, spinning prop would be like a barn door dragging at the wing, so, I'm sure, the power on the other three engines would have to be increased, just to keep the ship in the air. And that just increased the speed of that ailing propeller, until it eventually tore the engine, and sometimes a wing, off of the plane.

Rare? Yes, and I've only heard of two, personally, but sadly, they were both NW Airlines DC-7s, down in Southeastern Alaska, and, as I remember, only a week or a few weeks apart.

Would I fly in one of those beautiful, old birds today? You'd better bet I would. Just give me an invitation from some retired, old NWA, Minnesota farm boy, to go for a ride in a DC-7 and see how quickly I'd jump aboard.

The durability and dependability of those DC-7s were demonstrated in other ways as well.

My Dutch pilot friend, Cor den Hoedt (Cor the hat—"You know, hoedt, hoedt, like in Robin Hoedt," he admonished me one day), told me one day of climbing out of Orly in Paris, France on a dark, messy, torrential rainy night. Weather had said nothing about "embedded thunderstorms," thunderstorms embedded in other thick clouds. All four engines were at full power, so the carburetor heat (to prevent icing) was off. Suddenly, at about 4500 feet, they ran into a thunderstorm and terrible turbulence. The captain, flying left seat, immediately pulled the throttles back on all four engines, and immediately, in that heavy rain, all four carburetors iced up, and stopped all four engines. The captain shoved the wheel forward, and for a while, a Royal Dutch Airlines, DC-7, was a silent glider, somewhere in the night sky over the middle of France.

Very quickly, the engineer got one engine going, and very soon after, a second. The captain called for METO power, (Maximum Except Takeoff Power) and they could barely maintain altitude, which was now down to 2500 feet.

Shortly, the engineer got a third engine going, and that tough, old bird, that DC-7 could begin a slow climb, loaded though she was. A little later, the fourth engine took hold, and KLM, Royal Dutch Airlines, flying one of America's best, flew on to their destination.

Oh, tragedy was right there on their wing, but still, humor too. Cor said, "My gott, it was quiet in that cockpit for a few moments."

One more story, and we'll lighten up on the DC-7s. But, danger though there was, again there was humor, mostly in the way a Pilot spoke.

I was on the mike one night as a heavily loaded NWA DC-7, again, was lumbering home from TYO. He was about half way when he lost an engine. Sure, he still had three more. And pilots told me that you could expect to lose an engine once in a thousand hours. But since you had four, the chances of your losing two at the same time were maybe once in a thousand times a thousand hours. With the exception of those runaway props, I don't know of a DC-7 going down from losing an engine; that is, from an engine dying.

But this guy was heavy and at or near his maximum cruising altitude.

"ANC, NW 7."

"NW 7, ANC. Go ahead."

"ANC, NW 7. Please advise ATC, and Company (NWA), that we've lost an engine. We are close to our ETP (Equal Time Point) so will have to do some calculations, before we decide whether to continue on or return to TYO."

"NW 7, ANC. Roger."

I advised ATC, and sent a message to Company.

Shortly, "ANC, NW 7. Please advise ATC, and Company, we are returning to TYO. We'll need a new clearance to TYO. And ANC, will you advise ATC that we are unable to maintain altitude, but we'd like to hold what we can and let the ship settle slowly."

"NW 7, ANC. R."

I obtained his clearance for return to TYO, and his special clearance for settling slowly in altitude and delivered them to NW-7.

"And ATC requests that you report passing through each thousand feet," I added. We all knew that somewhere, closer to the water, that that tough, old bird would find dense enough air where she could hold level. But, with an airplane falling out of the sky, even if slowly, I understood the pilot's mild exasperation when later ATC asked:

"NW 7, ANC. ATC requests to know if you are declaring an emergency."

"ANC, NW 7. Well, advise ATC, we most certainly are."

But of course, they made it safely back to TYO.

You bet; I'd still fly in a DC-7 with one of those NWA, Minnesota farm boys any day.

But the DC-7s and Connies had to go. The DC-8s, Boeing 707s, and soon the DC-10s were prancing at the gate. And the Dutch were building enough cadre of Dutch boys that their need for other nationals was rapidly decreasing. (At one time, I was told, KLM had, in all parts of their operation, people from several dozen nationalities working for them.)

Bluie Salmon had been offered "The Golden Handshake," if he would resign. If he stayed, he would have to go through the long and rigorous training for the jets. But also, he had been thinking for some time of returning to his native Australia. So he accepted the not insignificant cash payment, and tendered his resignation. I can still see, clearly, in my mind, his final salute to me.

He had been to our house for a last visit. It was a day off for me. I had driven him to his hotel and, back home, became busied with some task, paying bills, I think, by a front, corner window. Looking up, into a bright, sunny day, I noted a DC-7, climbing out from Anchorage International Airport, about ten miles away. A common sight. But as I watched, that

DC-7 leveled out at about 1500 feet, and turned directly toward our house. He was not necessarily in violation of any flight rules, but it was clearly unusual to see a DC-7, still at that low altitude over our part of town, east of the Airport. I think Bluie poured on the power, and started his real climbout, just as that beautiful, old giant, roared low over my house, with such thunder that it shook the windows, and even the coffee cup on my table. Tears came to my eyes, as I cried out, "So long, Bluie; I know this is the end of an era in your life, but it is the beginning of another. So long, good friend."

He told me later in a letter, that as he cut off those big engines, there in Schipol, 14 or so long hours later, he felt like he was cutting off half his life. I understood, I understood. The jet era had come to the skies.

Photo courtesy KLM

A KLM DC-7, somewhere over Europe. Could this be that grand old bird who gave me her final salute in her last climbout from Anchorage International Airport?

CHAPTER 5

On the Beach

As I alluded to earlier, I left that really good job with FAA, early in 1965, and, as my beloved son said, "returned to the waters." The Alaska Department Of Fish And Game needed a captain for a patrol boat, over the "vast and endless reaches" of the Copper River Delta, and deep Prince William Sound. That was a dynamically adventurous time, and a dramatic story in itself. But you can read about it in my book, *THE COPPER SANDS*. It is really not a part of this story.

It had been "Plan A," as they promised, for me to do that job for the six months summer seasons and take the winters off, for the rest of my working days. But politics entered its ugly head, and the job was eliminated after that one season.

Ah yes, but again we can quote the Good Book, "It is not in man that walketh, to direct his steps." I was on the beach, and ten years flashed by as I worked at a number of jobs: driving a truck, managing the Alaska State Ferry System Office in Anchorage, running boats for world famous Foss

Towboat Company, and even carrying the mail, for awhile.

It was during this time that we very nearly lost our marriage. But through that storm, God led us to truly commit our lives to the Lord Jesus Christ. His peace entered our lives; we were "new creatures."

And then His leading prompted me to realize that I'd best start considering the not too distant issue of retirement. FAA had been a good job; they offered a good retirement.

But, John Bassler, who had been Assistant Chief of ANC FSS (Anchorage Flight Service Station) during some of my more rebellious years, was now Chief. He had a few reasons to not like me. I knew I'd have to get by John.

So one day, I put on my most sincere grin, and went to see John. I told him all, apologized for the past, and assured him that I was not the rebel he'd had to contend with, those years before. John, a devout Catholic, understood and readily accepted my assurances.

"No, Dean, I'll not only not block your return; but I'd urge you to come back," he answered. And then he added, rhetorically, "Why don't you go down to the R.O. (Regional Office) and see George Woodbury."

"George," I queried, "Why George?"

"Oh, he is *the* Personnel Officer for the Alaskan Region," he said.

George Woodbury—we had been the best of friends; back when we were both journeymen at ANC FSS. So I drove right down, and was soon seated in George's spacious office, and we were trading stories of the "good old days."

At an appropriate moment I said, "George, we are old friends, but I'll certainly not ask you to do anything special for me; you know that."

And he answered, "Dean, I couldn't, and I won't. But I appreciate the position you are taking."

But when I left, George followed me out into the outer room, where the rest of the personnel staff were working, and there we exchanged the parting banter. No, he told no one to give me special treatment. But no one in that room missed the unspoken message. In less than 30 days, I was again working for FAA. "The steps of a man..."

After four months of rigorous re-training at the modern, FAA Academy in Oklahoma City, I returned to Anchorage, but only to find that I was not allowed to be assigned to the Anchorage Station. I would have to be treated as a "new hire" and take a "Field Station" for a year, before "bidding" back to Anchorage.

But I was incredibly fortunate (or blessed?) to get Homer, a small, domestic FSS, near the southwestern tip of the famous Kenai Peninsula, and on that incredibly beautiful, Alaskan fiord, Kachemak Bay, bay of the smoke. It was an easy 220-mile drive on good roads, or little more than an hour flight by Twin Otter prop-jets, to Anchorage. Our paid-for home was in Anchorage; and my wife had a good job with the Alaska Dept. of Highways, a job we both felt it prudent to keep. So we kept two homes for that year.

Once I got settled in there at Homer, got to know the local pilots, and their delightful idiosyncrasies, it was a pleasant, easy job; and I would like to have stayed. But even there, an incident, one day, tied me back to the old E-459 days. I was working with Kim a beautiful girl, and a lovely human being. We had our "en route frequency" 122.2, switched to an overhead speaker, and our "airport frequency," 123.6, on a console speaker, so we could instantly separate them. It was quiet, we were chatting away about something. Suddenly, from the overhead speaker came, "Homer; KL868." We often heard the big birds calling Anchorage, over that speaker, so when I reached for the mike to answer, Kim tried to stop me, "No, no," she said, "That's not for us."

But I knew it was: "KL868, Homer, go ahead."
"Homer, KL868. Is Dean Nichols around?"
"KL868, HOM. Affirmative. Dean speaking."
"HOM, KL868, standby."

Photo courtesy KLM

"Up, up, up the long, delirious, burning blue..."
From the poem, High Flight. KLM loved the DC-10.

And then the familiar voice of an old friend, Dutch purser, Pieter Langerveld.

"Dean, this is Pieter. We'll be in Anchorage in just a bit. Can you get home?"

I answered that I couldn't, but I'd appreciate his greeting Alma for me, and petting my dog, Dusty. They both needed it.

We signed off; and there was beautiful, delightful Kim, standing there incredulous.

"You're *not* supposed to do that," she almost gasped.

"Well, I know, Kim. But shucks, he called me. I couldn't be rude, could I?" Like I've said, the "brass" knew we had to be human too.

Yes, I'd like to have stayed there in Homer, but— our home in Anchorage, and, my wife's job there.

So when an opening came at the ANC IFSS (International Flight Service Station) I bid on the position, and was chosen.

It had now been eleven years since I had been there, but when I walked into that radio room, there, spread out before me, was that same huge, old, familiar console, and the "Model 28" teletype printers. I felt like I was coming home. But it turned out to be the opposite of anything so easy.

CHAPTER

6

Re-earning My Wings

I'm a slow learner. A psychologist friend explained it to me one day. "It doesn't mean you're dumb; it is just the way your mental computer works. That computer demands that *all* the pieces be in place before you can grasp the package. That is why, when you do 'get it,' you become one of the best." And I did.

But the agony of that learning, and in this case, the re-learning process.

Many things had changed. As I said earlier, instead of 10 to 15 aircraft out there, there were now 30 to 40, or more. The time allowed for each contact was down, sometimes, to seconds. Much the same as before, a typical PSNRP, might still read, "FT 98 5735N 150W 1535 FL330 5745N 160W 1641 FR2001bs 280/135 -58." (Tiger [Flying Tiger Lines] 98 is 5735N [57 degrees, 35 minutes north latitude] 150W [150 degrees west longitude] at 1535Z [or Greenwich Mean Time, sometimes called Universal Time] Flight level 330 or approximately 33,000 feet. Estimating 5745N 160W at 1641Z. Fuel Remaining is two hundred thousand pounds. [Yes, that is 100 tons of fuel.] Wind is from 280 degrees at 135 knots. Temperature is minus 58 degrees.) It was from these hundreds of very abbreviated weather reports, incorporated into reports from steamships, data buoys, and other sources, that the National Weather Service is able to give us those remarkably accurate weather forecasts, especially out over that ocean.

It was those familiar PSNRPs that I copied so easily, as I sat at the training position on my first day back.

There were some there saying, "Wow, Nic's as hot as he was in the old days. He'll be soloing in a week or so." But it turned into a hard month, or maybe longer.

Photo courtesy Anchorage Museum of History and Art

E-459, the nerve center of ANC IFSS (Anchorage International Flight Service Station.) The operator, with earphones, is sitting at that Model 28 printer. The console to his left.

Those PSNRPs were no longer read back, but instead, were simply acknowledged by, "Tiger 98, roger your progress. Anchorage." And, the aircraft now gave a PSNRP every ten degrees of longitude, instead of each hour, so there was no predictable order. So they could bunch up, or scatter out; except during that four hours at dawn, when they were *all* bunched up, it seemed.

But even so, that PSNRP, though only acknowledged, would take close to a minute. The "servicing," (Frequency used, operator's initial, and such) would have to be typed in. And then the operator would reach over to the Addressing Panel and punch in the buttons for each of the three to five, or more, addresses to whom the teletype message (now waiting in the bowels of the old switching room) were to be sent. And then he would press the "Transmit" button, which would send the message on its way, but which, only then, would release his teletype printer to receive the next contact.

As I recall, there were some 85 addresses on that panel, and, although we had a "cheat sheet" above it, to use the sheet took far too much time, like five or six seconds, when one had less than two or three. So we quickly memorized them all. Typical addresses would be KSFOFT, or RJTTFT. (San Francisco Flying Tiger Lines, or Tokyo Flying Tiger Lines.)

Since the above sequence would take a minute, or longer, one could ask how 60, or that record 72 contacts an hour could be made. But many contacts were very brief, like:
"ANC, Tiger 98. Request 350."
"Tiger 98, roger, request 350. Anchorage."

or:

"Anchorage. JL402 level 390."
"JL402, roger, level 390. Anchorage."
Or, most clearances took only seconds to deliver. But I reiterate all this to show that there could often be three or four things happening at once. As an example: that JL402 could report level 390 while you were addressing the last PSNRP. It was very nearly always the same kinds of "things;" and so after awhile, the mind developed little compartments in which to tuck them while, say, the operator was addressing that last PSNRP. Then the brief item could be drawn from its "compartment" and put into the machine.

Simple, orderly, routine, and most exhilarating, *when*, the mental computer had all the "pieces" programmed into it.

But that "programming," that breaking-in, that learning process often was, and in my case, admittedly was, pure agony. Why would one subject himself to such agony?

Well, like a woman in childbirth travail: beforehand, one is certain it will not be all that bad. And afterward, the agony is forgotten but the reward is there.

The Japanese had their harassment by "environmentalists" too. You may recall the bombing, by some radicals some years ago, of the new traffic control tower, just before NRT (Narita Airport) was to open. Anarchy, I sometimes think is not so far away, but rather, the moral bonding of the social fabric holds order, but often only by a thread.

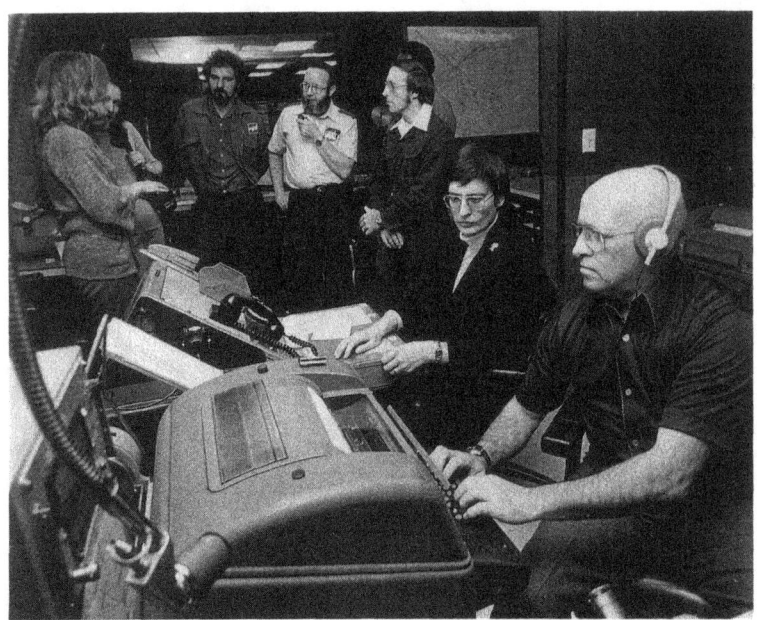

Photo courtesy Anchorage Museum of History and Art

The air/ground operator is taking a Position Report from an aircraft somewhere out over the vast Pacific Ocean. His assistant, at the "Interphone Position" looks on.

The tower was repaired, of course, and that needed, modern, new airport at Narita, Japan was opened. But the "environmentalists" did get the concession of a curfew on flights out of Narita during certain hours. As a result, and because of time differences, that meant a flood of aircraft out of Japan in our very early morning. From about 6:00 A.M. to 10:00 A.M., especially, things were really cooking at ANC E-459.

And into this environment, stepped the writer, and Jim Walcutt, trainees. Most fortunately for us,

Photo courtesy Anchorage Museum of History and Art

A secretary explains the "Status Board" to visitors. There are only around 18 aircraft listed at the time. The interphone position is in immediate forground. Note the necessary coffee cup, and, old, heavy duty time-stamp.

Wally Bedford was Watch Supervisor. Wally seemed absolutely incapable of believing that anyone could not eventually learn, and, be a good operator. And his record showed that result. I remember going to him, two or three weeks before I was "soloed," and telling him, with failure almost at the edges of my eyes, "Wally, I don't think I'm going to make it." He just listened, really understood, but gently, even very subtly had me back out, hammering on that "mental computer" programming.

But our principal instructor, Greg Repoff, was something else. Greg later became a good friend. I haven't seen him in some years, but I would really welcome a visit from him, so that we could relive some of those dramatic, tumultuous days. So I know Greg will just grin when he reads this.

But at the time, he seemed an arrogant, tactless, impatient brat. He was also a very highly skilled operator. It was Greg who made that record 72 contacts in one hour, alone. And I'm sure that he never got up a sweat.

All of us have some problem with trainees. Once *we* "get it," we forget the struggles *we* had in the learning, and wonder, "Why can't they see that?" But Greg was worse than most. He was so sharp, so skilled, so darned good, *and* so young, he was absolutely certain that these two "old guys," myself and Jim Walcutt, "will *never* make it." And that certainty dripped from him. I hated him for his attitude, but dared say nothing. Greg clearly held a mixture of contempt and pity for us. And I don't know which was worse.

Jim seemed even slower than I in the learning; but I don't think he was as torn up inside. He just doggedly held on, and that encouraged me. He wouldn't quit; how then could I? And eventually, Jim became, as Wally knew he would, a good operator,

Author photo

The Author at the aged E-459 Console, and equally aged Model 28 printer. Probably copying a "PSNRP" from one of his favorites, NWA Flt. 7, or "NW-7."
Anchorage, Alaska, Summer 1980.

and a gentle, capable, cooperative, and stabilizing co-workman—a real friend.

But for me came a morning, beginning the day watch at 8:00 A.M. The earphones were crackling with traffic. I was ordered to sit down in the primary position, with that huge console to my left. Greg took the printer and position behind me, with the console to his right. He could monitor every thing I did, heard, and said, and, help, if need be.

I don't know if any other E-459 operator would admit it, or not, but I was terrified. I even silently prayed, "Lord, get me out of here." But He didn't;

Re-earning My Wings

and anyway, how could a grown man be coward enough to run now?

We made it through those wild two hours, and the next day, and the next. One morning, Greg was away from that backup position, letting me literally solo, when traffic really got hot. He heard me give someone, "Standby, you are number five." So he sat down at that backup position, and started taking every other call, or clearance.

We could both hear, on our earphones, everything the other man heard, and what we each said. So, for example, when Greg would hear me say, "Varig 831, roger your progress," he would know I would have my "servicing" and addressing to do. So he would call the next aircraft, "Air France 271, go ahead."

When I heard him say, "AF271, R your progress," I would take the next, or give a clearance, or whatever. We got so busy, and had such a rhythm going, that I forgot all about being scared, but just flew with the eagles.

An hour and a half or so later, some of the aircraft went over to Seattle, some to ATC on VHF, and things quickly quieted down.

Finally, Greg turned around with a big grin on his face, and said, "Well, that was fun." And it was. His earlier contempt had been poorly hidden, but his new respect was equally as transparent. Agonizingly, the old skills had returned, but, they had returned. I had re-earned my wings.

CHAPTER 7

"The Steps of a Man..."

As these books have been written, I have found myself writing much about people. But, why not? People are alive, so unique, and, like snowflakes, although the same, are never the same. Each is another window into the mystery of mysteries—life itself, the wonder of life. How best to see one's self than through the eyes of another, and especially another of a different culture from our own?

I had joined a flying club, shortly after settling into Alaska, called, curiously, "The Opportunity Co-op Flying Club." They had two aircraft—one was a four-place, Aeronca Sedan, with a 145 hp Franklin engine. We flew it on skis, during the long winters, from the four-foot thick ice on Lake Hood, next to Anchorage International Airport, and on floats from the same lake during the short summers.

On floats, that Sedan was a dog, and on skis a little better, but most certainly not a Greyhound. But, it flew. One could explore the skies and the mountains, and the thousands, literally thousands of Alaska's lakes that could be reached only by the fragile wings, or, by long, long trudges across miles and miles of tundra.

The other ship was a very standard, 65 hp, Aeronca Champion, which we flew off Merrill Field, at the edge of the City of Anchorage (and where the Flight Service Station was located). We flew it on wheels during the short summers, and skis during the long winters.

It was off Merrill Field, with that Champ, on skis, that I had the opportunity to claim a dubious honor, twice.

On two different occasions, I took DC-7 Capt. Bluie Salmon for a ride in that Champ; and later, DC-10 Capt. Cor den Hoedt for a ride. A rare opportunity presented itself. I couldn't resist. Each time, somewhere during the flight, I turned to my "passenger" and spoke, with serious voice, but with a twinkle at the edges of my eyes, "Sir, I do hope you realize, that aboard *this* aircraft, *I* am the Captain." And each, in his turn, smiled, and gave me a respectful salute.

But how did we come to develop such fascinating, unique friends from those distant lands?

Well, my wife and I had talked of inviting one of the "foreign crews" out to our house for dinner sometime. One afternoon, we had come into Lake Hood with that lumbering, old Aeronca Sedan. As we were unloading, and securing the ship, three men walked up, and a conversation developed.

Noting their excellent English, but definite accents, we asked, and were told, they were crewmen from a KLM flight that had come in the day before. We told them of our interest in having a crew out to our house, sometime, but were not sure if they would care to come. But their answer was most encouraging. We couldn't do so at that time, but were encouraged by, "Oh yes, do so, when you can. Most any of the crew would be delighted at such an invitation."

Some days, or weeks later, as I worked my last shift for the week, I had noted that KLM868 had just flown in from TYO. So I drove downtown to the Travelers Inn and asked to see the captain of KL868. The desk clerk called down to see if the captain was in, and then directed me to his room.

A sandy haired man in his lounging robe opened the door and invited me in. As our conversation flowed, I noted that Capt. "Blue" Salmon had an accent, alright, but *not* a Dutch accent. I asked about that.

"Oh, I'm Australian," came the answer, "after the war, as KLM was expanding all over the world, they did not have enough Dutch boys to fly those big planes; so they hired pilots wherever they could find them. And not only pilots, but other workmen as well—dispatchers, office workers, maintenance men, mechanics, line crew. At the peak, KLM had a dozen or so different nationalities working for them."

(According to ICAO [International Civil Aviation Organization] rules, English *is* the universal language of World Commerce . If one were going to work for KLM, one *must* speak English. All control towers, centers, ground stations were required to operate in English.)

But Capt. Salmon and I were communicating in a most delightful way, so I asked, "And that nickname, 'Blue?'"

"Oh," he laughed, "My name is Henry L. Salmon; but in Australia, a redheaded man is always nicknamed 'Blue.' It is more natural to me now than my given name would be."

When I invited him, and his crew, to dinner, Bluie cautioned me, "Oh, you wouldn't want the whole crew. Let me select two or three to come with me."

And the next evening, I drove over for Bluie, his co-pilot, Cor den Hoedt, an engineer, and a stewardess.

An incredibly stimulating evening followed, as the conversation flowed like surging waves on the sea shore. We heard their stories of Tokyo, and Bangkok, and Karachi, and Amsterdam and Palermo, and Cape Town. And they listed as attentively as we told of Alaska, and tugboating on the Columbia River, and my work at E-459, from the ground radio man's point of view. But the rich, and startling revelation to us was the seeing of ourselves, our American culture, through those Dutch and Australian eyes. What rich, free, talented, blessed, big and open hearted people we Americans were through those eyes.

After I had driven them home, late in the evening, we talked of an incredibly rich experience. The "borders of our tents had been enlarged." We would never be the same again. And all this would not have happened, had I failed to master E-459. "The steps of a man..."

A Dutch crew did not remain together as a unit, but were dispatched on individual bases. So we lost contact with that kind and ruggedly Dutch engineer, and that stewardess. But as I remember, she was a bright, articulate, delightful woman. We missed her.

A month or so later, I noted Bluie's name on a KLM flight plan; so later I phoned him in his hotel. He readily accepted another invitation to dinner. I don't remember how we kept in touch with Cor; but somehow we did. After I literally talked to them like a "Dutch Uncle," I convinced them that "proper social manners" of them waiting for us to invite them, just would not work. They *must* phone us whenever they were in town. If we were unable to have them, we would frankly say so, no hard feelings. And it worked.

Some months later, Cor brought over a beautiful, Dutch stewardess, but who looked her French ancestry. Although I cannot recall her name, I believe it was French also. So let's call her Silvette. She was so quietly pleased to find a home that enjoyed having her around, that she came over often, when a flight brought her to that northern city. She would unobtrusively sit around, and play my records, and rest, away from the rousing parties most of the crew attended. She became a lovely friend.

One time, she brought over her purser, Pieter Langerveld. And another, instant bond developed. Over the years, Pieter became such a family friend that he often stayed at our home during those three-day layovers in Anchorage.

Many years later, after we had left Alaska, I was completing an around-the-world flight. I had written Pieter, that I would be arriving at Schipol on Pakistan Air; and I gave the flight number and time. "Can you pick me up, and drive me to a good hotel?"

As soon as I was in his car, the floodgates of conversation opened, as they always did with Pieter.

He drove away. After a while, he stopped in front of a row of fine looking, brick townhouses. "Is this good enough?" he asked.

My senses, dulled from the long, long hours in the air, I had some difficulty grasping the impact. But there, on the front door of one of the houses, was the large number, 40. Of course, Achterberglaan 40, Uithoorn, The Netherlands—the home of Pieter and Tine Langerveld.

I spent the next few days as their guest, in a real Dutch home. Such warm, return hospitality. After three weeks in Pakistan, the cleanliness, and order of that Dutch land refreshed my soul. I was eager to be home to America, *my* land; but the trail that had begun with my learning to fly after WW II, some thirty-five years before, had led to this clean and quiet place of rest. "The steps of a man..."

My Journal for one of those days reads:

"Thursday, January 12: Pieter came into my room just as I was awakening at eight-thirty—thirteen hours. A needed and most healing sleep. Pieter had a meeting down town, so Tine prepared my breakfast, Dutch style, two slices of bread with cheese and jam, and a cup of coffee. We talked awhile, and then she too left for town.

"I am alone now, in this so clean and comfortable (Spiritually, culturally *and* physically,) Dutch house, and looking out the window at the economy of Dutch buildings; and there are Dutch birds in the Dutch trees. Ah, but those are universal clouds in the Dutch skies. Who can order the wind, or the clouds they carry?

"A moment ago it grew very dark; the wind whirled through, and then the clatter of hail on the cobbled patio outside my window. It is clearing again now, with even some blue sky. A jet thunders over on its climb out from Schiphol a few miles away, and then the peaceful silence. This is not my land, but surely, this is second cousin to my land. I am at peace here for this much needed interval of rest in my voyage around the world.

"Oh the wonder, and yet the insignificance of jet travel. Cook, and Magellan, and Hudson are engraved in the stone of our history books, and they did their historic work at an average speed of perhaps less than three knots. Today, I am resting, relaxed, in a Dutch house in Uithoorn, Holland. Tomorrow evening, the schedule puts me in Boston, Massachusetts, with Ramona's sons, and the next day in Portland, Oregon, and Ramona's arms. And no one but Ramona and I, and a few friends and relatives will know, or even care. Ah, as I have said before, but we will know, and remember the marvel of the adventure of this voyage..."

"The steps of a man..."

But back to the adventure in Alaska. Cor retired some years after Bluie, and Pieter some years after that. We lost contact with Cor, and Silvette, that beautiful French-Dutch stewardess. But we still exchange birthday cards with Bluie and Pieter.

But two more brief stories that tell something of our experiences with those strong, beautiful "Dutch boys and girls."

Cor, and two or three crewmen from his ship were at the house one evening. My wife, Alma, was doing something at the kitchen sink, her back to us at an island, 4 or 5 feet back. Cor finished his drink,

Photo courtesy KLM

Although the Dutch Crewmen knew the "far-away-places-with-their-strange-sounding-names," their by far favorite was Alaska. "What an experience."

and then, for fun, tossed the remaining ice over her shoulder, and into the sink. Of course, she yelled, and then began to laugh. But a storm of Dutch erupted from the other men. And Cor answered in defense. And then, in English, he further defended himself with the words, "I know my limits in this house." Those guys were indeed, real gentlemen.

One time, we had taken Pieter, and a stewardess, by the name of Rene', to our cabin for a weekend. It was some 60 miles by road, and then 10 miles by our fast, twin-engined runabout across the lakes and through the channels to the cabin. As we were racing back down the lake to our car, on the last day, Rene' said, with evident wonder, "What an experience." We viewed our own position with new respect, and even awe. "The steps of a man..."

When Bluie Salmon went home to Australia, with his three beautiful children and his Dutch stewardess wife, Miep, he realized one of those lifelong "dreams," and bought a 900 acre ranch near Dandenong, in the state of Victoria. Bluie was a worker and rebuilt a ranch that had been quite neglected and run down.

I still have copies of the colorful letters he wrote of that rebuilding process. But as that ranch grew in productivity, those long letters lessened. Finally, one admitted, "I never realized how much free time those aircrews had."

But I'm glad they did. Because of that, our own lives have been incredibly enriched. I sincerely believe that all of that experience was no accident, but rather indeed, "The steps of a man..."

CHAPTER 8

Odd Stories—Somewhat Related

Margaret Brown

"Blessed are the peacemakers, for they shall be called the children of God." Matt. 5:9

And this lovely woman, capable co-worker, true friend, was all of that. She was indeed a peacemaker. A beautiful, tall, shapely, black woman, she was almost exactly the same age as my oldest daughter. When they both stormed through their 40th birthdays, I openly laughed at the incongruity. These "girls" were now in their 40s, while I was the same age I had been for the last 20 or 30 years. They laughed with me.

Margaret was a good operator; not outstanding, but a good operator. She didn't hesitate to ask for help any time she felt she needed it. But neither did any hesitate to help her. If her own duties were not too demanding, she kept a gentle eye on the others, and just quietly stepped in to lighten the load. It was infectious.

Our crew had settled down to five, in the latter years—Wally, our supervisor, Jim Walcutt, Phyllis, Margaret, and myself.

The work itself tended to build tensions, and the work seemed to attract people, like myself, who were a bit "highstrung." But, when Margaret came into a room, peace entered with her. And with that peace, God's Agape Love, warmth, respect, and a spirit of ready cooperation.

There were four positions in the ANC IFSS, E-459, the Air Ground Radio Position; the IFO, or Interphone Position, or assistant to the radioman; the Telephone-

Photo courtesy Anchorage Museum of History and Art

In my book, *A Poet's Sketch*, is the story, "Fam Trips are Worthwhile." Margaret Brown and I shared that "Fam Trip" aboard this very FAA, C-123, itself now retired. She is taxiing down a road, on which she had landed, to be delivered to Alaska's Air Museum in Palmer.

Photo courtesy Anchorage Museum of History and Art

The FAA, Federal Aviation Agency, Alaskan Region, finally retired a faithful workhorse, the rugged C-123.

Flight Plans-Teletype Position; and the International Weather Broadcast Position. We were normally assigned to two hours in each position.

I remember one night when someone had to leave for a few moments. Margaret just stepped in and took over. When the one came back, such was the spirit of oneness, they just stepped into the vacant slot; and that repeated a number of times. Somewhere, later in the watch (Midwatch, I believe), Jim looked up and announced, "You know, I don't believe any of us are in the positions assigned to us." We all grinned, agreed, and decided, "Oh, I suppose, we should take our assigned positions."

Truly, we were a motley crew, but with this quiet, strong, lovely woman there, we blended together in a spirit of unity that can make any otherwise nominal group into a team of champions.

A Good Cook

It got so that we all actually looked forward to Midwatch, or The Graveyard Shift, as some called the shift from midnight to 8:00 A.M. A miserable time to be up and working, while most of the normal world was fast asleep. And, as I've said, the shift wound up its last two or three hours in a storm of activity. But, there were compensations. There was no "brass" around, no office or other staff to compete for the kitchen in the "Rec Room." And, generally, things were fairly quiet for those first five hours or so.

"Time for a feast, Phyllis," someone would announce. High strung, even feisty at times, Phyllis didn't seem to belong there. Her rhetoric spoke of home, and cooking, and interior decorating, and sewing; and her knowledge and talent in those areas was evident. But why was she there?

"Oh," she said one day, "I just wanted to see if I could do it," and she did. Again, not outstanding, but she did her job as an Air Traffic Control Specialist.

"Why me," she demanded, "why do *I* always have to do the cooking?" And the chorus would answer, "Because you're the best cook." And she was. Grumbling, she would head downstairs to the kitchen. The three of us would willingly step in and pick up the load. We knew that beneath that mildly crusty exterior, was a mother's heart. And an hour later, up the stairs would come Phyllis with steaming pots of truly gourmet food. The "brass" didn't need to know the intimate details. We got the job done, and well. And morale? On our team, it was the finest.

The Battle of the Sexes

I can't let those two fine women off without this story being told.

It was a quiet Sunday afternoon, I believe. The morning rush was over. There was time for talking. Phyllis was at the radio, Margaret at Interfone, and I over by the teletypes and phones. The "girls" were talking, woman talk, mostly. I was paying little attention, but rather, was watching small planes landing and taking off out on Merrill Field.

But then I started picking up on a theme in their conversation. They were agreeing on the fact that they'd rather work with men than with women. Some of the reasons they were giving each other were quite different, but that common theme recurred again and again, "Oh yes, I'd much rather work with men than with women."

Now, before some Feminist gets on my case for being a male Chauvinist (there are female Chauvinists too, you know), let me remind her, I was not speaking. These were the words of two, very real women.

But after half an hour or more of that, a thought came to me. I spoke; and they both turned to listen.

"You two ladies have reiterated a number of times," I said with measured speech, "that you'd rather work with men than with women. But did it ever occur to you two women that so would we?"

There was silence for a bit; they both grinned and changed the subject. And that's all I'm going to say about men and women working together on identical jobs.

Oh, there was no injury to our friendships. As I said, these were real women.

A French Joke

Air France was beginning their own polar flights. I don't know if this was the first, but certainly one of my first contacts with the French.

From somewhere up around Point Barrow: "Anchorage; AF 271."

"AF 271; Anchorage; go ahead."

"Anchorage; AF 271; we have a commissary order. Are you ready to copy?"

"AF 271; Anchorage; ready to copy."

"Anchorage; AF 271; Commissary order: fifteen bottles of white wine; twenty-four bottles of red wine; twelve bottles of Muscatel..." and the order went on.

I read back the message.

"Anchorage, AF 271. Readback correct."

I sent the message to Company.

I never again took such a message. It was some years later that we realized it was all a French joke. I can hear the conversation on that flight deck, as that big plane droned on high over the northern ice. "Those crazy Americans think all Frenchmen are 'winos.' Let's call in a 'wine order' for him." And so they did. And I, faithfully but a bit gullibly, took and relayed the message. I'm sure that I can hear the laughter on that flight deck, and later, at dispatch on the ground.

But that's OK. They were good guys and neighbors on the planet. I was, however, given the opportunity to get my own laugh at the expense of the French, as told in the next chapter. E-459 was a fun job.

A Miss Is as Good as a Mile

The Nenana Ice Pool is a tradition, almost as old as Alaska. I don't know when it began, but certainly many, many years ago, betting began on when the ice would break up on the Nenana River, up near, or south of Fairbanks. A tripod was fastened to the ice out on the river and a wire run to a big clock on the shore. As the spring melting occurred, and the ice began to move, the tripod would move with it, pulling the wire, and stopping the clock. The person, or persons who had guessed the month, day, hour, and minute, would win the cash prize, somewhere over $100,000, as I remember. I believe the most common time was early May, but April times had won, and some June times too. We always bought a dozen one-dollar tickets, just for fun. A federal law had made such "gambling" illegal, but Alaska was an exception, because the Nenana Ice Pool had become such a tradition.

Capt. Bluie Salmon had wanted to get in on the fun, and had bought, in our names, a few tickets.

A friend in electronics maintenance had shown me how to slip into the "Frame Room," in the next room, and plug a local radio station into a switch on my console. When things were quiet, I could flip that switch and listen to music or the news.

It was late May; the ice was ready to go any minute at Nenana. The dramatic tension was mounting, as a reporter at his microphone right there in the "Clock Tower" was describing the scene; and I was hearing all on my ear phones.

Meanwhile, Bluie Salmon, Captain of Royal Dutch Airlines Flight 867, was out west of Alaska, on his way to Japan, but still in contact with me. I had the times of all of our tickets on a slip of paper, but Bluie's were the only ones close—one, only ten minutes or so away.

The tension on the wire, and in the reporter's voice, was increasing; the clock was ticking. "I don't know why the clock has not stopped," he was almost shouting, "the ice has moved, the tripod has moved, the wire is tightening. It should go any second now."

It was Bluie's month, day, and hour; and let's say, he had the time of 2:28 P.M. And, I had a precise chronometer on my console. "Twenty-five," the reporter counted off, "Twenty-six, oh, oh, the tripod moved a bit more, that wire is singing. Twenty-seven—twenty-eight." Bluie's time.

I almost hit the foot pedal to call Bluie. But then I saw our clock, and heard the reporter shout, "Twenty-nine, 2:29 P.M.; the clock is stopped; this year's Nenana Ice Pool is over."

I let up on the foot pedal, and started to breath again. I don't remember if I called Bluie and told him how close he had come, but I think I did not. It would have been an illegal transmission, of course, and for what.

But had that clocked stopped one minute sooner, I think even the Director of the Federal Aviation Administration, Alaskan Region, would have just smiled if I had called, "KL 867, please advise Capt. Salmon that we just won the Nenana Ice Pool."

We only missed by one minute, but, as it is written, "A miss is as good as a mile."

Slips Don't Count—But They Do

One early Spring ice of another sort probably cost Japan Air Lines much more than those winnings of the Nenana Ice Pool. Anchorage was experiencing one of it unusual "Silver thaws," as we called them on the Columbia River. It was raining, and freezing as it hit. Wet ice. There is nothing more void of friction than wet ice.

A Japan Air Boeing 747 was taxiing out, taking a taxiway the mile or so to the end of a main runway. "That taxiway has not yet been sanded," the Tower warned. But with a combined weight of fuel and aircraft of close to 200 tons, the captain felt he could make it safely.

Easing down that runway at 1 or 2 miles per hour, he crossed a small gulch where a fill had been made to keep the taxiway level. But there must have been the slightest of slopes there, because that big, ungainly bird started to slide, turned part way around, and slid off, backwards, into that 40 or 50 foot deep gulch, breaking its back, tearing off some engines, and doing much other damage.

As I recall, no one was hurt, physically; although I wonder if that pilot ever recovered from such loss of face.

And I'm not even sure that the aircraft was able to be salvaged.

Somehow, the telling of this story makes me a little sad.

Isn't that like life. Sometimes the smallest slip, can count so very, very much.

B-747 photo courtesy JAL

Every Airline has had its tough breaks. JAL had theirs
But over the years, they developed an outstanding Airline.
And their radio gear was the best. Can you imagine Sony, or
Hitachi being anything else?

Odd Stories—Somewhat Related

So now, let us end this chapter with a few lighter stories, "somewhat related" to the N.P.M.W.A.R.A.

The Propeller Is Fine

In the early days, before the microwave relay systems were perfected, so that flights up over the north Canadian islands could reach their relay stations on VHF, we had a ground station at Pt. Barrow. It was "manned" by several Eskimo girls. They were not so very busy, but they did a good job.

I had in my home, and still have, the beautiful, old, Sensenich wooden propeller I'd had on a 1946 Taylor Craft. Cor den Hoedt had fallen in love with it. But of course, I wouldn't part with it.

But a few weeks later, I was able to buy a beauty from an old-time airplane mechanic, Jake Bryant. I can't remember if I paid $5, or $25, but it was a steal. On his next trip through, we gave the prop to Cor. He took it home aboard a DC-10. As he carried that wooden propeller aboard that huge, jet airplane, a few looked at him incredulously. He blithely answered, "Yah, just a spare, in case."

Late that evening I was on E-459, and heard one of the girls at Point Barrow working KL 868. (Spoken KLM 868), up over the Pole. I couldn't hear the aircraft. So I asked Point Barrow to ask KL 868, "How is the propeller?" She hesitated a bit, but complied with my request.

"KLM 868; Point Barrow. Anchorage requests to know, 'How is the propeller?'"

I could not hear the answer. But shortly, "Anchorage; Point Barrow. KL 868 says that the propeller is fine," (or flying), I couldn't tell for sure. But that was fun. I know those Eskimo girls pondered that curious request for a long while.

Just Never Thought of It

The 1964 earthquake knocked out most of our frequencies—smashing some electronic equipment, but mostly knocking over antennas.

The day after, I was assigned to E-457, the Air Ground Position that used those HF frequencies, as mentioned earlier, to work the aircraft down the offshore route to Seattle. But on E-457, the frequency, 8871, was working well, and, curiously, or by God's Grace, we were able to talk directly to Seattle; something almost never possible in the daytime.

Quickly, word got around, and in between aircraft contacts, I had a series of requests to ask Seattle to phone relatives in the States that so and so was safe and OK. Rules and protocol were thrown to the winds. We just did what we could to help.

But I never even thought to ask Seattle to phone my own brother, so *my* family there could know about us. *We* were OK. It was those others who needed help. When telephone service was again restored, my brother reminded me of my oversight. But I just never thought of it.

Priorities

But let's end this chapter with a serious story. About 6:00 o'clock, one evening, I was on E-459, plugging away at the light traffic. A Pan American World Airways Boeing 747, PA-5, called:
"Anchorage; Clipper 5."
"Clipper 5; Anchorage; go ahead."
"Anchorage; Clipper 5. Can you give us the status of the Series? (World Series baseball games.)
"Clipper 5; Anchorage; standby."
I turned to our telephone man. "Can you call one of our radio stations, and find out the status of the World Series?" I asked.
Surprisingly quickly, he had the data in my hand.
"Clipper 5; Anchorage. Message."
"Clipper 5; go."
"Clipper 5; Anchorage. The message reads: 'Third game, bottom of the 7th; two out; Yanks leading three to one.'"
"Anchorage; Clipper 5. Copy OK; and thanks, Anchorage."
Those Clipper pilots *could* be nice. And anyway, this *was* a priority item.
I almost think now, that perhaps this story should have been in Chapter 10. It isn't just "somewhat related," it was the "heart of the job."

CHAPTER

9

Fam Trips—and Other Stories

The Boarding Fee

SF-160, the "Standard Form, number 160," was the form we completed when we wanted to take a "Fam Trip," (Familiarization Trip) in the cockpit of a commercial airliner. Ostensibly, the purpose was to give us firsthand knowledge of the operations on the flight deck of the ships we aided by radio in their voyages across the seas and over the land.

And we did learn much, even a few things we probably should not have known. But we did learn. Of course, the only time FAA would let us go for such a Fam Trip would be on our own time, like, say, we would be flying to Seattle, or Portland, or Philadelphia on our vacation. No one objected to "doing it on our own time." After all, there was a considerable dollar saving in air fare. We were guests of the airlines. And the flight crew were generally good sports about it all, even though they did have an FAA type looking over their shoulders.

Curiously, I knew of no more than two or three pilots who made "Fam Trips" to the radio room of the ground station that *could* mean their life. But then, we couldn't carry them from point A to point B, for free, either. But, who could knock a good thing? And the airlines were wise enough to work at the good will of those who served them.

I had seriously considered bidding on a transfer to Sitka, halfway down the panhandle of Alaska. Wally, who was recommending me to his old chief there, urged me to take an "SF-160, Fam Trip" down there for a visit with the chief. As I was waiting in the terminal for boarding for the return trip, I met the captain and his co-pilot of Alaska Flight 101.

"So you are the one riding jump seat with us back to Anchorage?" he asked.

"Yes, I am," I answered.

"Fine; there is no charge, of course, for the flight. But you are aware of the $25 boarding fee we charge for pickups at these intermediate points; are you not?"

He was serious, yet, just a bit too good-natured.

I hesitated for a few seconds; and then answered with the same mock seriousness, "Yes, of course, Captain; you will take a personal check, won't you?"

We laughed together, hard. They were good guys.

There *was* one thing that I learned, riding all over the United States in the jump seats of DC-10s, Boeing 747s, 727s and others. Those flight crews, almost to a man, were devout capitalists, very right wing politically, and strongly anti-feminist. We got along just fine. They would have appreciated the sub-chapter, "Battle of the Sexes."

And I remember, one time, riding down the Columbia River aboard an Eastern Airlines, B-727. As we hit the Columbia at the big bend, where the Snake enters the Columbia, I began a travelog of the points of interest, on a world famous waterway I knew so well. They were delighted, and listened with close attention. I knew our presence in their private domain was an intrusion. But for this while, I felt truly welcome. Truly, it is more blessed to give than to receive. SF-160, Fam Trips—I miss them still.

Photo courtesy Eastern Airlines

Reversed roles: The passenger gives the travelog to the crew.

Sometimes You Just Have to Fly Them

Anchorage International Airport, and I was quietly sitting in the jump seat of a DC-10, listening to the flight crew go through their pre-flight check lists. Occasionally, the response would be, "No, it's not working."

"Try again," the captain would say.

"No, it is still not working."

"Well, OK; go to the backup. But note that on the report."

The DC-10 is a most remarkable ship. There were two of almost everything. And sometimes, backups for backups. Still, I was poignantly aware of the number of items for that report.

Finally, the captain, I suppose sensing my mild apprehension, turned to me and said, "We just bought this ship, and three others from a non-sked outfit that had had them mothballed for a couple years. Our maintenance people have gone over them thoroughly; but they just can't find everything. There finally just comes a time when you have to just start flying them, and find the problems as you go."

Well, I appreciated the logic. But I was secretly assuring myself that, of course, he was not including on that list such items as engines, and controls, and wheels, and wings.

Regardless of the very few problems with DC-10s that the news services have typically blown out of all proportion, Douglas built a superb airplane in that DC-10.

In fact, Capt. Cor den Hoedt told me that he has ridden a DC-10 that was programmed to take off from Schipol Airport in Amsterdam, fly itself over the Pole to Anchorage, set itself down, and taxi to the off-loading ramp. Of course, hands were ready to intervene at any point. "But that aircraft was fully capable to do that," he said.

What a vast leap in technology that is, from the not so long ago, "early days," when DC-7s, flying over the Pole, carried a fourth man on the flight deck, the navigator. When necessary, they could, and often did, take star sights with a sextant, and worked out the incredibly complex mathematics to determine their position, up there over that lonely, and icy desert.

An Embarrassed Pilot

Of course, sometimes it was not the equipment at all, but a foolish oversight, so common to man.

It was a glorious day; visibility at least 135 miles. An SAS, DC-8, was coming in from Europe. He contacted the tower, made his approach, landed, and taxied to his dock.

Then he called the tower. "For your information," he said, "Your VOR is stuck on 111 degrees."

VOR stands for VHF, Omnidirectional Radio Range. It sends out a double signal, and the receiver measures the micro-second difference in time between the two signals. From that variable difference, the receiver tells the pilot what direction he is from the radio range transmitter, and whether he is right or left of the selected course to that range.

Although it was a glorious day, with, as I said, almost unlimited visibility, they had tuned in the ANC VOR, just as a cross check.

"What frequency are you tuned to on that VOR?" the tower asked. And the pilot gave the frequency.

"Sir," the tower responded, "That is the frequency for the 'test' VOR. It always remains at 111 degrees, so you can check the accuracy of your own equipment. The frequency for the ANC VOR is..." And he gave the frequency.

An embarrassed pilot for a world known, national airline, acknowledged, "Ah, yes, you are so correct."

And passengers, filing off the airplane, and by the open door to the flight deck, made such kind remarks as, "Thank's for the ride," or, "See you next trip," or, "That was an excellent landing, Captain."

And the captain just smiled, and thanked them for their courtesies.

Photo courtesy SAS

SAS, Scandinavian Airlines System, is truly one of the great airlines of the world. They are just human, like all the rest of us. And they have a sense of humor. An early DC-8 on the Polar Route.

77

Photo courtesy SAS

SAS too, moved up to the B-747 on the Polar run to Tokyo.

Photo courtesy SAS

And also the rugged DC-10.

CHAPTER

10

Odd Stories—Heart of the Job

A Walk in His Moccasins

No one, who knows the inside stories, would minimize the incredibly highspeed complexity of the work in the darkened rooms of an Air Traffic Control Center, or, I think, even more so, in the exposed, lofty floor of a busy control tower. I have heard that Chicago O'Hare is the busiest airport, and so the busiest control tower in the world. And so, I was told, the controllers work for two hours on and two hours off, two hours on, and two hours off. The work demands such intense concentration, that the human machine can do no more.

No, I would not minimize any of that. But somehow, the books, and movies, and T.V. stories have dramatized those centers and towers, but missed the also very real drama taking place in the supporting communications network.

We were an extended arm of the airline companies, yes, but the dramatic part of our work was the sharing with ATC, the work of following the flights of those hundreds of metal birds around the skies. We directed their paths, to some extent, protecting them from each other, being their lifeline, their electronic umbilical cord to the earth, to which they *must* return. And we were doing all that with that unique, *noisy*, often fickle, but most useful HF radio.

As I have said before, that E-459 Console looked like the flight deck of a Boeing 747. Sitting at that durable, old console one day, probably close to 18 years after its birth, I counted up over 150 indicator lights, buttons, switches, and dials,—that were no longer in use. I have no recollection at all of the exact number that *were* in use, but it was considerable. But, like the flight deck of that big ship, really, only a few demanded attention at any one time. It was the demands for rapid decisions, that made the job exhilarating, and challenging.

I remember one time, when someone had an idea, a good idea. And for some time, controllers from Anchorage Air Traffic Control Center, were assigned to two-hour stints as observers at E-459. A couple of those boys would sit with us with a pair of earphones on, and listen, and watch our work. Never, did one of those boys leave, without some clear evidence of new respect for E-459. "I don't know how you do it; I just don't see how you do it," we often heard.

As too often happens, the program fizzled out after awhile. But it had made its impact. We seemed to work together better after that.

And, as I have also said, I knew of no more than two or three pilots who visited the radio room of E459. But one evening, my friend, Capt. Bluie Salmon, spent a few hours with me there.

"You know," he confessed to me later, "I used to often get impatient with the ground stations, and let that impatience show in my voice—until I went over there with you. I just never realized; I had one aircraft to deal with at a time; you have 30 or 40."

Fam Trips—a program badly neglected, and which could have so abundantly oiled the machinery of the entire Air Traffic Control System. What is that Proverb? First Indian 1:1, "Do not judge the other Indian, until you have walked a mile in his moccasins."

A Helping Hand

Anchored far down in the Gulf of Alaska, was a Canadian weather ship, Ocean Station Papa. They also provided some radio link and navigation support to ships, and, to some extent, to aircraft. We shared some HF frequencies, although we seldom had contact with each other.

This day, signals were not impossible, but they were not good. Traffic was not heavy, but it was steady. I received a call, on 8939, I believe: "Anchorage; Ocean Station Papa; we have a Canadian Air Force 101, that is flying out to check on us, but we can't raise him. Will you see if you can get a PSNRP from him for us?"

Of course I would, and went to work. As I'd said, signals were not at all good, but I finally raised him on 8939. It took some work, with many requests for repeats, but I finally pieced it all together.

Probably, 10 or 20 minutes had flown by, I don't remember; but during that time, our own aircraft were calling. I just about had it all put together, and Wally heard me say, "Tiger 97; Anchorage; standby, you're number 8."

Startled, he stepped over and asked, "You need some help?"

But I grinned and said, "Oh, maybe; but I've just about whipped this problem," and called Ocean Station Papa to deliver the PSNRP. But an elated Canadian sailor came back with, "It's OK, Anchorage, I got it all on your readbacks. He'll be contacting us on VHF in a little while. But thanks for the helping hand, Anchorage."

Wally sat down at the backup position, and, working as a real team, we cleaned up the traffic backlog, and E-459 settled into its normal rhythm. "Never a dull moment," on the N.P.M.W.A.R.A.

H.Y.

I've never met this man, in person, but through those nebulous radio waves that reached across the sea, channeled "between the heavens and the earth," a real friendship grew. Somewhere in my files I have his name, I think; but through the never ending pressures of time on us all, I lost what little letter contact we had.

His identification initials were HY. Mine were DN. Often, we would hear TYO (or they us) working an aircraft; and we would copy the PSNRP on our own printers. As soon as we heard him break off the contact, we would cut in with, "TYO; ANC copies JL304."

And he would answer, "ANC; TYO; roger." And we would both know that I would route the teletype message to all American addresses, saving that much teletype traffic across the sea.

But more times than not, we could not perform that service, and so the teletype messages would come in for our information also. There, on the servicing, would be the initials of the operator on duty. We quickly learned to identify each other's voices with those initials, especially HY and I.

HY was a superb operator, and obviously full of zeal for the job. We thought alike, and often understood each other, even without words. Many, many times, I would sit down at that console in the morning, the earphones crackling with traffic. After the first contact, or three, TYO would say, "Is that you, DN?"

"TYO; ANC; affirmative. HY?"

"ANC; TYO; affirmative," and I could hear the grin in his voice. And we would go to work.

I say, without apology, that I had gotten good by that time, really good. But I wasn't as good as that gentle, kind, most helpful and cooperative, and incredibly skillful, Japanese man. He kept me on the edge of my chair, just to stay with him, but I would not have missed that challenge for all the world.

Somewhere in that far away nation lives a man with the initials of HY. And as the old memories come flooding up from the almost forgotten wells of my mind, I realize that we were more than friends, those long years ago. We were brothers.

Just World

After that deeply moving story, (Well, I don't know if it was so to the reader or not, but it surely was to me in the writing.) but after that, as they say in stage dramatics, now we need some "comic relief." Almost everyone knows the names of such scheduled airlines as, Pan American World Airways, Northwest Orient Airlines, American Airlines, Eastern Airlines, United Airlines, and on and on. But there are many, many, maybe hundreds, of "non-scheduled" airlines, referred to in the system as non-skeds.

I had never heard of World Airlines. And, in the very early days, was a bit naive.

One evening, I received a call from WO720, World Airlines flight 720. I gave him reporting times, as we did with the old "paddle wheelers." But at each contact, although he referred to himself as World 720, I thought he was just abbreviating his ident. Since the only "World" Airline I'd ever heard of was TWA, Trans World Airlines, I would respond with "Trans World 720, roger," or "Trans World 720, that is affirmative."

Finally came an exasperated call, "Anchorage, FYI (for your information) this is *not* Trans World. We are World; just World." And I can see the look on that pilot's face, even now.

And with a sheepish grin on my own face, I responded with, "World 720 Anchorage. Roger, understand, just World."

What Are *You* Doing on *My* Private Line?

Once in a while, a serious problem, with its funny side, would appear; and it would have nothing at all to do with sun spots, or the solar wind, or radio equipment, or accents. It would just be "Spring Breakup" in Anchorage, Alaska.

Understandably, we had to have instant and reliable communication with ATC, over in a secure enclave furnished by Elmendorf Air Force Base. We were situated at Merrill Field, a few miles away.

But there were those two hundred million dollar airplanes up in the sky, loaded with 200 or more living souls, all traveling at over 500 miles per hour. They needed information from the earth, often in seconds. And ATC often had only seconds to give a clearance, or warning, to one of those "Argosies with magic sails." It was imperative that we have a "private line" to ATC.

The Anchorage Telephone utility, of course, had their, mostly underground, lines all over the city. So FAA naturally rented lines from them. And that worked well, most of the year.

But that was before air pressured lines were developed; and well before waterproof gel impregnated lines were developed; and years before fibre optics lines, no way affected by water, were developed.

But, again, in those early days, when spring breakup came in Anchorage, the deeply frozen ground would allow no water to soak harmlessly on down into its depths. So that rapid runoff found every crack or crevice it could, and slipped in. Those buried telephone lines were vulnerable. And water would raise all hobb with those copper wires, carrying the delicate electric currents that were our voices with their cryptic, but vital messages.

One wet, spring night, in those early days when we did our own interphone work, I had called ATC. A woman's voice came on, "Hello, hello."

I responded with, "Mam, this is a direct line to the ARTCC. I don't know how you got on here, but please hang up."

The indignation that poured into that earphone was fluid, and cutting, "Me hangup. I'll have you know this is a private line. What are *you* doing on *my* private line, young man? Now you just get off of here, and right now."

As so often happens, with old stories from the past, I don't remember how we resolved that serious-funny problem. But I think we used a regular phone line for awhile. The airplanes kept flying, and safely. And eventually, the deeply frozen earth thawed, the lines dried out, and an indignant "lady" and I were properly separated.

These things only happened once a year.

Murder?

Accents, of course, can be a problem in any communication, but with the frequent static interference, and sometimes distortion on those unique HF frequencies, those accents could be a *real* problem.

But as we learned to communicate with those men from many lands, we quickly discovered that we could readily adapt to the accents of the Dutch, (KLM), the Germans (LH, Lufthansa), and the Scandinavians, (SAS, Scandinavian Airlines System) and yes, even the Australians. But the French, and Japanese, and Koreans were much more difficult.

Someone explained that, although there are many French words, and even a few Japanese words in the English language, that basically, English is from a Germanic base, and thus the ease with which we adapted to those others of a Germanic base.

I joked a bit about "even Australian." One time Bluie Salmon brought another pilot friend, Eric West, a real Englishman, out to our house. We got to talking about languages, and accents.

"Oh, you Americans devastate the English language," Eric told us, "But the Australians murder it."

You know, I do remember receiving a telephone call from Bluie one time, a few years after he had returned to his homeland. I could hardly understand him. Murder? Well, I don't know. But there was considerable distortion, I must agree.

I know that when Bluie reads this, he will grin a big, wide, Aussie grin. But I'd have to remind him, *he* gave me a not-so-small Australian/American dictionary.

Growls In My Earphones

"Anchorage, Varig 831."

Every syllable was enunciated with great care, and so were easily understood. But I would have

Photo courtesy VARIG, Brazilian Airline

A VARIG MD-11.
Growly voices or not, they were a fine airline.

Photo courtesy of VAR

A VARIG B-747.
They flew some fine aircraft.

known it was a pilot for the Brazilian Airline, if he had said, "Good afternoon, Anchorage."

Every one of those pilots—(they didn't come through too often) but every one of those pilots spoke with the same deep, growly voice. I don't know if they were born that way, if the Amazon did something to them, or if they learned that from each other. But every one of them could have qualified as a movie star with those unique, growly voices.

And then, maybe the Amazon women in that land... Well, they were fine pilots; they did their work well.

Remember The Wine?

Remember when the French had a good laugh at my expense?

And I said that was OK? Which it was. Well, then we could agree that perhaps I could be a bit justified for returning the favor.

In the earlier years, both the French and the Japanese were having real difficulty with English. Later, both improved, much, the Japanese especially.

But during those early years, one night, when traffic was light, but signals horrible, I was listening to AF271 trying to get a message over to TYO RDO. The harder each tried, the worse their English became.

Now I know this was serious, and yet it was funny, and I laughed, even while being a bit sobered by the fact that each was still doing a better job of speaking English than I could with French, or Japanese.

But the punch line came when, in desperation, one of them shouted, "Spika Englis, spika Englis."

And the answer came, "I am spika Englis; I am spika Englis."

I apologize for laughing, my friends; but, remember the wine?

The Universal Language

There is an interesting footnote to the last story. I was told the following by a pilot who often flew into Quebec, Canada.

Although, as I have said, English *is* the universal language adopted by ICAO (the International Civil Aviation Organization), the French, who dominate the province of Quebec, had ramrodded through a special regulation that, in Quebec, the pilot could use *either* French or English. And so they did, for a short time—less than a few months, I believe. But it was the French pilots themselves who wisely put a stop to the practice.

Much of the information that comes into a busy pilot's mental computer around a busy airport comes to him through the radio exchanges he hears between the ground and the *other* aircraft. A pilot who speaks no French, and you can't fault him for that, comes in, in the above cases, half blind. He hears radio exchanges, but they have no meaning to him. Too many near-misses occurred. And the French speaking pilots, themselves, were wise enough to demand the change back.

There are some good reasons why English must be the universal language. And even such great poets as Kalil Gibran, an Arab who has chosen to write in English, says, in effect, "English gives the writer, and speaker, greater freedom to express himself. It truly is a universal language, even with all its flaws."

But the simplest, and best reason for ICAO choosing English as the standard, is safety. With often only fractions of seconds to make a decision, we *must* have a common understanding. Those wise, French pilots knew that.

Tough Going

The Koreans came into the high flight later in the game. And so, of course, can be excused for having some difficulties that the rest had already mastered. But like myself, slamming back into E-459, with only memories of the old, easier flowing days, the Koreans stumbled around for awhile, just trying to play the game.

Their English was passable, but for a time, their radio maintenance was abominable. Time after time, it seemed, a Korea Air B-747 would leave the VHF frequencies with ATC and try to come over to us on his way along the northern airway back home; and we would lose him. Many times, busy as we were, we'd have to ask another aircraft within a few hundred miles to contact him on VHF and relay his

The N.P.M.W.A.R.A.

747 photo courtesy Korean Air

Korean Air is, today, a highly respected airline. We all stumbled much, in our beginnings. The story only illustrates another of the problems we struggling radio men had to solve.

PSNRP. It worked, but that was *not* according to system design. Skirting down along the edge of Russia, it was there that KO-007 flew over Russian territory by mistake and was shot down.

Less tragic, but potentially as dangerous, was a bad habit we discovered some Korean pilots had. They would request to climb, say to FL350. We would pass the request to ATC.

Often, for all aircraft for that matter, due to the crowded airways, ATC would be unable to grant the request. We would receive the advisory:

"CA KO 005, UN 350." (ATC Advises Korean Air 005, unable to approve FL 350.)

But, not understanding English all that well, as yet, and, with poor signals, and with poorly maintained equipment, the pilot would hear only what, perhaps, he wanted to hear, the number 350. And the next PSNRP he would report at FL350; not at all where ATC expected him to be.

So we asked ATC to change those advisories to read, "UN higher altitude." That worked much better. No numbers were spoken.

But if the Korean radios were the worst, Japan Air radio equipment was by far the best. Well, can you imagine a Sony or a Hitachi *not* being the best?

Oh, the Koreans came along OK, later in the game. But with the storming game they entered, they made it a bit tough going for us, for awhile.

Gratitude in the Night Sky

As more of these stories come up out of the deep wells of my memory, I'm thinking that perhaps I should not have been quite so hard on those Pan Am pilots in my earlier stories.

Most of the Japanese radiomen were good operators, and that HY was truly superb. But, they had to have trainees on once in a while too. One dark night (Aren't they always "dark nights?") I heard Pan Am, Flight 5, PA5, coming out of TYO for SFO. He was one or two thousand miles out of TYO, but still in the Japan Control Area. He was trying to get higher altitude from TYO. But time after time he would get only, "Roger, request 350; standby, standby." But no clearance came.

Some time later:

"TYO, Clipper 5; are we going to get higher."

"Clipper 5; TYO. Ah, standby, standby."

I don't know how long this went on, but an hour or more, I'm sure.

Finally, from PA 5:

"TYO; Clipper 5; C'mon man, get on the stick. If I don't get higher pretty soon, I'm not going to get from where I am to where I'm going."

But again, from TYO Radio:

"Clipper 5, TYO. Roger. Standby, standby."

I could just see that pilot, turning to his flight engineer, "John, are we going to make it home?"

And the engineer's answer, "No, not if we have to eat up all this fuel down at this altitude."

But I knew that the aircraft was coming up on 165E longitude, the boundary between TYO Control Area, and ANC Control Area. So I had a clearance ready for him. As soon as he called with his crossing of 165E, I came back with:

"Clipper 5, ANC, ATC clears Clipper 5, CTAM FL 370"

"ANC; Clipper 5 is cleared to FL370; we are leaving 330" He was ready for a 4000 ft. climb. And the grateful relief of that frustrated pilot breathed over the airwaves to me. Those Pan Am pilots were good guys.

A Beautiful Bird

But those "slightly superior" Pan Am pilots could be "cool Dudes" too. Remember that NWA DC-7, settling out of the sky after losing an engine? Well, that's pretty serious, when an airplane won't stay in the sky. Of course his answer to the question from ATC, "Are you declaring an emergency?" was, "I most certainly am."

(There must have been other Pan Am flight numbers, but for some reason, I can recall only two, 3, and 5.)

Anyway, I think it was in the full daylight this time, I heard:

"ANC; Clipper 5. Will you advise ATC that we are shutting down an engine. We'll be a little late on getting to our next position."

"Clipper 5; ANC; roger."

I advised ATC.

A few moments later, my IFO man handed me a request from ATC:

"Clipper 5; ANC; ATC requests to know, are you declaring an emergency?"

And from Clipper 5, came the unconcerned answer: "Oh no, Anchorage, we just shut down an engine. We just thought ATC should know."

Those incredible Boeing 747s had power to spare, and, a shut-down jet engine was no where near the drag of a runaway prop. It couldn't even have one.

In fact, although there was, of course, some drag to any appendage on the outside of an airplane, those engines were so streamlined that the innovative Dutch, at least, had some of their 747s fitted with special hangars so that they could carry a spare engine, out on the wing between the two in use. Once in a while, an aircraft in, say Japan, would need a new engine. So here would come KL867 with a fifth engine on the wing. It was the easiest and most economical way to get it there, even if some questions were asked, like, "When did 747s start operating with five engines?" Boeing built a beautiful bird in that 747.

Life's Surprises

Remember the stories of the curious behavior of those HF frequencies once in a while? A number of times, it seemed, we would hear Aeroflot, a Russian Airline flight somewhere over Siberia, trying to raise TYO. If the signals were skipping badly, we would hear them loud and clear, but TYO would hear but silence.

So we would call, and sometimes take a PSNRP, and relay it back to TYO on teletype. But I remember the interesting, slightly disturbing feeling at knowing that I had stepped over the border into a Communist country. Suddenly, that boundary did not exist. Like migrating birds to whom a line on a map means nothing, those radio waves were stopped by no line a man can draw on his charts. He was a bird in the sky, with a need to weave another thread in that nebulous umbilical cord with the earth.

Less often, we would hear that twangy Australian accent. One night, like Bluie Salmon trying to raise Amsterdam, I heard a Qantas aircraft calling Sydney. There was no answer, from Sydney, but he sounded "right next door" to me. So I called him, and offered to take his PSNRP. I of course, didn't know the three letter identifiers of his present position and estimated

Odd Stories—Heart of the Job

Photo courtesy Aeroflot

A huge, heavy-lift cargo carrier, this IL-76 can work off of the many dirt and gravel strips in the vast land that Aeroflot serves. Aeroflot generously sent us over 20 excellent photos of their fleet. Space will allow us to reproduce no more than two.

Photo courtesy Aeroflot

The long range IL-86. Could this have been the "bird in the sky" we gave assistance to, one long winter night, so long ago?

Photo courtesy QANTAS, The Spirit of Australia

QANTAS claims to be the oldest airline in the English speaking world. Well, they claim to speak English, murder or not.

position, so he had to spell them out. But we got it all, and relayed it down under via teletype.

I wonder, did my experience with the accent of that Aussie-Dutch pilot, help me that night with one of his countrymen, six thousand nautical miles away?

Life, so full of such exhilarating surprises.

The Weatherman Was Right

One winter afternoon, AF 272, was coming in from TYO. A few hundred miles out, he called and asked for ANC weather. I gave it to him, which included, ceiling 200 feet, visibility 135 miles. There were a few moments of silence, and then:

"ANC; AF 272; please confirm ceiling 200, visibility 135."

Why there is no "U" in Qantas.

In the beginning,

we named the company Queensland and Northern Territory Aerial Services, Ltd., even though it consisted of little more than a one-room office, a wooden shed, and a single biplane carrying farmers and graziers through the skies of the Australian Outback.

Now, more than seventy years later, Qantas Airways has mastered the art of making long distance travel seem noticeably shorter. And easier. Qantas features one of the youngest, most modern fleets in the world.

As the oldest airline in the English speaking world, Qantas strives to be the best. Today's Qantas has an enviable safety record, the respect of other airlines, and the loyalty of thousands of passengers on five continents.

The original name has long since lost significance except as a reminder of brave and difficult origins, which may be why we feel such affection for it. That's why we are not being merely perverse when we pronounce it "Kwontas" but spell it QANTAS.

The Missing U.

Well, it did seem a bit incongruous, a cloud ceiling as low as only 200 feet, and yet the visibility over 100 miles; but I repeated the weather report, "Ceiling 200, visibility 135."

There was a longer pause, and then I called AF 272, and explained: "Sir, there is a level ceiling of 200 feet over Anchorage, that extends only a few miles north. Out from under that level ceiling, we can see Mt. McKinley, gleaming in the bright sun. Mt. McKinley is 135 miles north of us. So the weather report is correct."

"ANC; AF 272; Ah, roger. Thank you very much."

Well, he was being duly cautious. As we all know, the weatherman *can* make mistakes.

He Didn't Say That

Two more NWA stories, and we'll let up on my good friends, those solid old Minnesota farm boys.

Back in the earlier days, a heavily loaded NWA DC-7 was lumbering west, intending to stop at Cold Bay, far out on the Alaska Peninsula, for refueling. CDB was more in line with his great circle route to the Orient and some 500 miles or so closer to his destination.

He was somewhere south of us when Dispatch sent a teletype message for him. I called, and read it to him: "Reports from CDB state that the temperature at CDB is 33 degrees. The wind is directly across the runway at 40 knots, gusting to over 50 knots. The runway is covered with wet ice. Braking action is nil. Suggest you divert to ANC. Do you concur?"

Sarcasm is too strong a word to use on those solid old farm boys. He answered, "Anchorage, NW 3; advise Dispatch that, yes, I most certainly do concur. We are diverting to ANC."

But I could clearly hear an unspoken message which read, "Good Grief, Dispatch, with conditions like that, there would be no way on earth I could keep your airplane on the runway. What do you think anyway, man? Of course we'll divert to ANC."

But he didn't *say* that. He was one of those Minnesota farm boys.

Old Friends

I don't know where Flying Tiger Lines found all of their pilots for those steady old freighters, lumbering with daily precision across the North Pacific Ocean. But they were a bunch of "cool cats" too.

Photo courtesy Tiger Retirement Club of Los Angeles

A freighter in the skies.
Flying Tiger's freight version of the versatile B-747.

Time has a way of stealing some of the details of memories, so I don't remember if this was my contact, or it was told me by one of my fellow operators.

But calmly, over the airwaves, came the call:

"Anchorage, Tiger 98; would you advise ATC that we have another Tiger out here, flying formation with us? We really don't mind, but we thought it was a bit against the rules."

It must not have been my contact, because I don't know how it was resolved, or even how it happened. But obviously, some misunderstanding had occurred. No harm was done. At those altitudes, it nearly always was crystal clear; they were flying the same direction. And VFR pilots do the same thing every day. But I suspect that some controller was feeling a bit sheepish, as he unscrambled that "glich," and cleared one or the other up or down two thousand feet.

Photo courtesy Tiger Retirement Club of Los Angeles

A C-54 carries the famous Tiger name which is no more. Federal Express bought them out a few years ago.

So far as I know, Flying Tiger Lines is one of the most successful freight hauling airlines.

"Well," a Tiger captain was telling us one day, "The reason you don't see painted Tigers, is pure logistics. The paint on a 747 will weigh about 480 lbs. That's equal to a quarter ton of freight. And on a few thousand trips, that's a lot of ton-miles we are being paid for that don't cost us a dime to haul."

Flying Tiger Lines—I never did get a "Fam Trip" with one of them, but they are right in there with NWA, in that warm spot in my heart one holds for old friends.

Lice—A Poignant Drama

This story is in no way a reflection on a people. If you or I were escaping from the hell that was Vietnam, we might have some curious infections too. But the desperation in a Boeing 747 captains voice was certainly understandable, and, something to hear.

"Anchorage; NW 7; Company message."

"NW 7; ANC; go ahead."

"Anchorage; NW 7; will you please see that NW Airlines in Seattle, *and* the Public Health Service in Seattle, receive this message." And with measured words, he spoke: " '*All* Vietnamese aboard are infected with lice. As a consequence, the *entire* aircraft is infected with lice.' Please see that this message gets to NWA in Seattle, *and*, the Public Health Service in Seattle. Let me repeat the message." And he repeated it, word for word.

"ANC; NW 7; may I have a readback please."

Signals were good. That NWA radio was working well. That captain was enunciating without flaw. He just did not want me to miss one word.

I gave him his readback.

"ANC; NW 7; readback correct, 'The *entire* aircraft.' And please see that NWA, *and*, the Public Health Service in Seattle *get that message.*"

We teletyped the message to NWA, and, since we had no teletype link with PHS, we telephoned them in Seattle.

That captain was desperate, and *so* helpless. I really felt for him. Lice are extremely hard to get rid of. The captain could not throw anyone overboard, or hose down the ship, crew, and passengers with salt water, as an old sailing ship captain would have done, or strip everyone and burn their clothes, as an army colonel might have done.

He was sealed into a metal tube with a couple hundred other souls—some angry, and perhaps with mutinous thoughts as helpless victims, and others helplessly aware of the unspoken resentment flowing their way.

I cannot begin to understand the thinking on the part of the NWA official who sent back the following message for NW 7. When it came in, I read it, and then looked up at Wally Bedford, our supervisor, standing in the doorway.

"Wally, would you deliver this message to NW 7? I've, ah, got to go to the restroom."

Wally read the message, just smiled, and said, "Oh, you're already working the aircraft. You go ahead."

I knew that pilot could not kill me through those airwaves, but I had to brace myself as I called: "NW 7; ANC; Company message."

"ANC; NW 7; go ahead." I think I heard a scratching sound in the background; but it might have been static.

"NW 7; ANC. Company message reads: 'Please advise which parts of the aircraft are infected with lice.'"

I don't, for the life of me, remember what happened after that. Maybe the aircraft just went up in smoke; or maybe the captain was overpowered by the crew and put in a straight jacket. But whatever, business over the N.P.M.W.A.R.A. continued on as usual.

It sure seems like we've had a lot of stories about NWA, and NW 7 in particular. But that is why they are often called Northwest Orient Airlines. They've been flying around the North Pacific Ocean for a long time.

And I really didn't want to tell this story. We've told of airplanes losing an engine and falling, if slowly, toward the sea. We've told of aircraft diverting because of impossible landing conditions. We've told of aircraft finding themselves at the wrong altitude, or in an illegal formation flight with another aircraft that was not supposed to be there.

But I just felt that the intense poignancy of this drama would not allow it to be left out.

If we had not blocked Vietnamese General Ky from invading the northern half of *his* country, and thus reuniting that hurting nation from the south, we would not have had the blood bath, and mass exodus, that followed the ending of that war. Nor would we have had to tell this story. But, this is not a political book; we'd better leave that to the historians. But this night...

In all of the training manuals at ANC IFSS; in all of the training manuals at Northwest Airlines; in all of the training manuals on flying Boeing 747s, I know that there is not one word on what to do in such an impossible situation.

I'm sure that that captain, crew, and passengers, all survived. But I hope that the captain reads this, one day, and he will know, that one man, in a radio room, on a dark night, in Anchorage, Alaska, truly suffered with him through his desperate dilemma.

Northwest Orient Airlines—You know, I believe I have reservations to fly with them to TYO, and on to Manila this coming April.

CHAPTER 11

The Final Story

I suppose that one might conclude, after reading all these stories, that all was one crisis after another on the N.P.M.W.A.R.A. Of course it was not that. These stories were scattered over more than eight years. Obviously, there were many, many days and nights, some quiet, but some busy with smooth flowing rhythms of PSNRPs and clearances, with weather exchanges, and Company messages fitted in here and there.

But it truly, truly was a dramatic, challenging, if demanding job. I would not have missed it for anything.

But in the early days, when E-459 first came into being, it was but part of the FSS, the Anchorage Domestic Flight Service Station. But after awhile, several of us were assigned, almost exclusively to that International Air/Ground. And that was excellent. We became specialized, and truly expert. And, the public, the pilots, were well served. Oh, it often meant eight hours straight at that microphone and printer. But that was OK. We developed a smooth rhythm that flowed.

Between my first and second stints at FAA, the station had been split into two, the domestic FSS, and the IFSS, or International Flight Service Station. And the IFSS had those four positions, as mentioned earlier, but all centered around, and related to, E-459, the Anchorage link with the skies over the North Pacific Ocean.

Although that scarred, old console, and those twenty-year-old, Model 28 printers were still doing their jobs, and well, our ties to ICAO demanded that we go full computer operated. And so the work began to install that equipment, or the terminals for that equipment, downstairs in the heart of the FSS. At the same time, the two stations were re-combined, and all ATCSs (Air Traffic Control Specialists) were expected to rotate between *all* positions.

That was not just a mistake. It was a terrible blunder. One might be working for a week with the small planes, thinking as they thought, feeling as they felt, working with swallows, dipping into the lakes and ponds of the wild land. And all of a sudden, one would find himself at the computer terminal, expected to fly with the eagles. It was impossible to keep honed, those finely tuned skills.

Oh, that doesn't mean that there is no benefit in a DC-10 captain coming home from a flight and unwinding by taking his Piper Cub for a flight into the mountains, or his small boat for a day of gunkholing along the coast. But the same thing that made those diversions a restful benefit was the same thing that interfered with the professionalism we

The Final Story

needed to truly flow with the rhythms of the big birds. We had to think like *they* thought, feel like *they* felt, to be truly one with them. And with daily work experience spread so thinly, that could not be done.

As the computer terminals were installed, and the slow phase over began, I saw that I was facing some of the same dilemma that my friend, Capt. Bluie Salmon, had faced as the jets took over. He was too near his planned return to his native land to start a new career.

And I didn't want to go through another training agony on the new computer keyboards, and "CRTs." That twenty-year-old console and those Model 28 printers and I had become old friends. If they were wanted no more, then perhaps I should leave with them.

So I had a good talk with the Station Chief, Jerry Ball. Jerry was young, but he was hard. But somehow, he and I had come to like each other. Maybe respect, would be a better word. We respected each other's minds. We had our usual "head game," but after a bit, he smiled, and agreed, "Sure, Dean, if you are going to retire in just a few months, it would indeed be redundant to spend the time, and expense, training you on the new equipment. I'll tell your supervisor."

But there was one more thing that made retirement look better all the time. Although I am definitely not "anti-union," I do have some difficulty with some aspects of the unions. And I really don't want to tell this part of the story. But I feel that the safety of the flying public demands it.

Anchorage Station was not a "closed shop." That is, one was not compelled to belong to the union in order to work there. As a result, only about 60 percent of the ATCSs were members of the union. But the union did have the exclusive right to set the kind of watch scheduling used. The "Rattler" Watch Schedule was introduced. Only union members voted. And 60 percent voted for the "Rattler." Sixty percent of 60 percent is 36 percent. That meant that 36 percent of the ATCSs at ANC FSS forced the remaining 64 percent to work that "sked," whether they wanted to or not. Oh yes, the ANC ATCC (Air Traffic Control Center) had been working it for some time; and I am amazed that someone has not sued FAA, for allowing such mentally stressed, poorly rested people to work daily at jobs that demanded refreshed bodies and alert minds.

And what is a "Rattler," or Accelerated Watch Schedule? After a man's two days off, he came in on his first watch, or work day, at 4:00 P.M.; the second watch at 2:00 P.M.; the third watch at 8:00 A.M.; the fourth watch at 6:00 A.M.; and the final watch for that work week at midnight that night. Of course his bowel rhythms, his eating rhythms, his sleeping rhythms, were a shambles by then. "But look," the *young* men extolled, "You have what seems like four days off, and it only costs you two." Like some young people using drugs, these boys were actually believing, "We can handle it."

The hedonistic philosophy was not for me. Ram through the work week any way you can? Get it done with, so that the *important* things in life could be given more time? No, no; they had their priorities, their sense of values totally reversed. It was time for me to retire.

I had been left upstairs to man that old console, while the new computer equipment was phased in. But that inevitable day came, when we were needed up there no more.

During a break, one afternoon, I walked up to that venerable, old radio room. That old console was still intact. As I stood there, listening to the quiet hum of the equipment, saw the few glowing and blinking lights, the silent dials, a curious sadness gripped me. No one sat at that grand, old Model 28 printer; no hand would control those switchboard dials, no voice would speak again through that waiting mike. An inanimate object? I think not. She was a living thing, but one meekly waiting her death.

And though I saw no one, I felt the presence of the spirits of the many men whose voices had passed through the wires of that scarred, old, gray console, both transmitting and receiving. An era had ended for me too. I understood, even more deeply, the sad, depth of finality that Bluie had felt when he cut off those big engines for the last time.

I laid my hands on those old machines, and, with the tears of parting at the edges of my eyes, said goodbye, and walked back down the stairs.

Sometime, during my last stint at E-459, an electronics maintenance man had found, in a storage room, a pair of earphones identical to the raunchy looking, but excellent old phones most of us had preferred to use. The ones he found were not on the records anywhere, so he gave them to me as my personal pair.

When I left FAA, I brought them home. And now, hanging on a peg in my den, those funny looking, old fashioned appearing earphones crackle no more with the static from the Northern Lights, nor with the accented voices of those men from many lands.

But those old phones speak to me, every now and then; and I almost feel my foot reaching for the bar that will key my mike:

"Northwest 7 — Japan Air 304 — Varig 831 — KLM 868 — Clipper 5 — Air France 272 — Lufthansa 403 — Tiger 98 —World 720 — Korean Air 007 — Alaska 302 — Scandinavian 130, this is Anchorage. Go ahead; you are loud and clear. Go ahead, sir, we read you loud and clear."

Epilogue

During those last few months, I had begun dreaming this dream: "When I actually retire, maybe I can move back to my beloved Columbia River, buy a small tug, and play with small towing jobs for the rest of my able life."

Maybe. But who knows? Who really knows? For is it not written? "The steps of a man..."

Glossary

FSS	Domestic Flight Service Station.
IFSS	International Flight Service Station.
IFR	Instrument Flight Rules.
VFR	Visual Flight Rules.
ATC	Air Traffic Control. Usually spoken, A.T.C.
ARTCC	Air Route Traffic Control Center. Often spoken on a callup as just, "Center..."
R	Roger, or, I understand and acknowledge your transmission. Spoken, Roger.
C	ATC Clears...
CA	ATC advises...
UN	Unable.
RL	Report leaving...
RR	Report reaching...
CTAM	Climb to and maintain...
FYI	For your information...
FL370	Flight level 370; approximately 37,000 feet. Spoken, Flight level three, seven, zero, or sometimes as just three, seven, zero.
ETP	Equal Time Point. The point somewhere midway in a voyage in which, considering winds and other factors, it would take equal time to go on, or to return to the departure point.

RDO	Radio.
SKED	Schedule.
SKEDD	Scheduled.
IFO	Interphone. The "Hotline" to the ARTCC.
PSNRP	Position report.
OPNML	Operations normal.
ARPT	Airport.
PHS	Public Health Service
ANC	Anchorage International Airport. Usually spoken, "Anchorage." Rarely, "Ank."
TYO	Tokyo
CDB	Cold Bay, Alaska.
HOM	Homer, Alaska.
SEA	Seattle.
PDX	Portland.
SFO	San Francisco.
GMT	Greenwich Mean Time. The time in Greenwich, England, and used by all International flights. Sometimes it is called Universal Time, or Zulu time. It is usually shown as a 24 hour clock, and, for example, 1735Z. Aircraft anywhere in the world are thus all on the same clock. Translation is done locally.
NWA	Northwest Airlines.
NW 7	Northwest Flight 7. Spoken, Northwest se
JAL	Japan Airlines.

Glossary

JL 304	Japan Air flight 304. Spoken, Japan Air three, zero, four.
VG	Varig Airline, the Brazilian Airline.
VG 831	Varig Flight 831. Spoken, Varig eight, three, one.
KLM	Royal Dutch Airline.
KL 868	Royal Dutch Airline flight 868. Spoken, K.L.M. eight, six, eight.
PA	Pan American World Airways.
PA 5	Pan American flight 5. Spoken, Clipper five.
AFR	Air France.
AF 272	Air France flight 272. Spoken, Air France two, seven, two.
LH	Lufthansa, Germany's Airline.
LH 403	Lufthansa flight 403. Spoken, Lufthansa four, zero, three.
FTL	Flying Tiger Lines.
FT 98	Flying Tiger Lines flight 98. Spoken, Tiger ninety-eight.
WO	World Airlines
WO 720	World Airlines flight 720. Spoken, World seven, two, zero.
KO	Korean Airlines.
KO 007	Korean Airlines flight 7. Spoken, Korean Air zero, zero, seven.
ASA	Alaska Airlines.
AS 302	Alaska Airlines flight 302. Spoken, Alaska three, zero, two.

SAS	Scandinavian Airlines System.
SK 130	Scandinavian Airlines System flight 130. Spoken, Scandinavian one, three, zero.

www.ingramcontent.com/pod-product-compliance
Lightning Source LLC
Chambersburg PA
CBHW050833160426
43192CB00010B/2012